DATE DUE

The Hesburgh Papers

The Hesburgh Papers

HIGHER VALUES IN HIGHER EDUCATION

Theodore M. Hesburgh, C.S.C.

ANDREWS AND McMEEL, INC.
A Universal Press Syndicate Company
KANSAS CITY

The chapter "Education in the Year 2000" originally appeared under the title "Making Prophecies of our Goals" in *The Third Century,* copyright © 1977 by Change Magazine Press, NBW Tower, New Rochelle, New York 10801.

The chapter "The Moral Purpose of Higher Education" originally appeared in the *New York Times*, copyright © 1973 by the New York Times Company. Reprinted by permission.

Library of Congress Cataloging in Publication Data

Hesburgh, Theodore Martin, 1917-
    The Hesburgh papers.

    1. Catholic universities and colleges — United States. 2. Education, Higher — United States — Aims and objectives. 3. Academic freedom. 4. Church and college — United States. I. Title.
LC501.H44   378'.01'0973   79-10408
ISBN 0-8362-5908-4

CONTENTS

SECTION THREE
Special Concerns in Higher Education in Modern America

SECTION FOUR
The Years of Campus Crisis

SECTION FIVE
The Future: Church, Education, World

Introduction

All of this book is directly or indirectly involved with values in higher education, and, beyond that, with a special but not exclusive focus on Catholic or Christian higher education and the Catholic university. This is not unusual because this is the world in which I have spent all of my adult life. One learns as one lives and as one learns, his philosophy begins to develop. This does not happen in a year or a decade. In my case, it has been happening since I first came as a freshman to the University of Notre Dame in September of 1934, at the age of seventeen. I have never since that day lived outside a university, although I have lived in several here and abroad and have visited hundreds all over the world, on every continent. I first saw Latin America in 1956 and Africa in 1958 by visiting practically every important university in every country where there was one. It was a wonderful introduction to each continent as I saw them through university eyes for the first time. I had earlier done the same in Europe and have since visited many universities in Asia, the Philippines, Indonesia, Australia, and New Zealand. The same for Russia and other socialist countries.

I have learned about universities and higher education in this pleasant way, but also through hundreds of books and, especially, through a lifelong experience of associating with wonderful university people, administration and faculty, and, of course, long generations of students, who justify and, I hope, vindicate all of our efforts.

Over the years, one's philosophy of education grows and becomes more precise and detailed. What I wrote fifteen years ago I would hardly write today. And yet, it may be helpful to sense the progression in thought and expression. Very few educators sit down and put their philosophy of education together in an orderly whole. Rather, we are forced by circumstance and invitation to outline this or that aspect of the process, speaking to students, fellow educators, and the public at large. Gradually, the philosophy takes shape. There is considerable overlap in the process. One is also somewhat at the mercy of what one is invited to do on this or that occasion, requiring a new expression, the development of another aspect of the whole. Fortunately, there are also occasions when one is challenged to look at the whole process and consider education or the university or one's task within it more comprehensively.

Gradually themes develop. This is especially true when one speaks to students about what one comes to believe should most importantly happen to them in the process of education. But even these central themes are differently expressed as one's own experiences bring newer and clearer insights regarding the goals of education. In the light of a changing world, one comes to understand better the key issues involved.

Nine years ago, at the height of the student revolution, I took a trip around the world to get away from it all, to see some new places and to regain my equilibrium and second wind. Before leaving, I tossed most of my educational papers into a flight bag in the hope that I could put some order into the mass during the trip, especially since I was taking the first part from Los Angeles to Sydney, Australia, by boat. Unfortunately, the day I left, July 4, 1969, President Nixon's two lieutenants, Robert Finch of HEW and Attorney General John Mitchell, announced that they were abandoning administrative action for court action in the matter of achieving integration of schools and other civil rights goals. In view of the relative efficacy of the two methods over the previous fifteen years, this was like trading a Cadillac for a pair of roller skates. For the first week or so at sea, I was writing furiously on the subject. The result was so incandescent that I never published it. Then came preparation for a public lecture aboard ship, calls at exotic South Sea ports, press conferences in New Zealand, and, alas, when we arrived at that beautiful harbor of Sydney, I had hardly skimmed the educational papers. From then on, they were so much excess baggage. But I did arrive back at Notre Dame rested and exhilarated and ready to write many more pages about the heightening crises, both in education and in civil rights. So the pile grew and the years passed.

Last summer, *mirabile dictu*, I was able to block out two quiet weeks in the north woods of Wisconsin for some fishing and reading and thought. Once again, I filled the flight bag, now twice as large, with educational papers. I spent the first week, a few hours a day, just reading them. Since I write my own words and do my own research, I found myself repeating phrases here and there. I like to think that I found some growth and development in the main themes, too. At least, they get more concrete, specific, and detailed as the years pass. I believe there is a consistent theme of values running throughout that may make my central concerns for universities, faculties, and students more meaningful for anyone interested.

I found myself wanting to interpolate here and there, but most often resisted, because I felt each paper should reflect honestly the situation at the time it was written.

It is always difficult to know where to begin, especially when one sits at a long porch table covered with papers, distracted by the beautiful, tree-fringed lake out beyond, birds singing, clouds floating, water lap-lapping, and all the rest.

I shuffled and reshuffled the papers, discarding more than half of them, my idea being that each paper should take a step further or elaborate a particular theme a bit more. Still, where to begin? Finally, I decided to begin with the two most recently written papers, not precisely because they were the most current of papers spreading over a decade or so, but because the first reveals me more clearly than the others. Somehow this sounds immodest, and I do not mean it in this sense. Rather, it seemed that anyone reading what I have to say about higher education in general and Catholic higher education in particular should have some idea of where I ＿ what I think of my role as president of Notre Dame, ＿rceive leadership to be. If I have no clear idea about ＿ is no profit in reading further. Everything I ＿ point, with a clear emphasis on

The second paper, the most recent of all, gives an overview of American higher education, where it has been and where it seems to be going. Again, this is the world I mainly inhabit and most of what I say pertains to the values that make this a very special world indeed.

In the various chapters that follow, I have tried to speak mainly in the second section to what has been the central endeavor of my life, the formation of a great Catholic university in modern America, and the problems and opportunities of Christian higher education generally. All American higher educational efforts, as universities worldwide historically, began with the churches. This is approached both comprehensively and in detail. I hope that one cannot read this first part without acquiring some sense of how I feel most deeply about the subject.

The third section is of broader scope because I am here mainly addressing myself to special problems in all of American higher education, again with special emphasis on values. It will be obvious to the reader that those broader concerns to which I was attracted and in which I became involved on the national or international scene, such as science and technology, human rights, human development, and values, began to loom larger in how I thought about higher education everywhere and anywhere, beyond the purely Catholic context.

The fourth section is a special approach to what has to have been the most interesting, difficult, and challenging period in my forty-four years as a student, professor, and administrator in higher education. Several times, at about two-year intervals, during the worldwide student revolution of the late sixties and early seventies, I had to pause and take stock, to try to understand what was happening and what we might learn from the experience. I believe that each time I learned a little more, and at the end was able to pull together the total experience. It also seemed appropriate to offer a case that may be of historical importance should we eve kind of crisis again. It is easier to forget hard to learn from them.

Finally, in the concludin

education and in civil rights. So the pile grew and the years passed.

Last summer, *mirabile dictu*, I was able to block out two quiet weeks in the north woods of Wisconsin for some fishing and reading and thought. Once again, I filled the flight bag, now twice as large, with educational papers. I spent the first week, a few hours a day, just reading them. Since I write my own words and do my own research, I found myself repeating phrases here and there. I like to think that I found some growth and development in the main themes, too. At least, they get more concrete, specific, and detailed as the years pass. I believe there is a consistent theme of values running throughout that may make my central concerns for universities, faculties, and students more meaningful for anyone interested.

I found myself wanting to interpolate here and there, but most often resisted, because I felt each paper should reflect honestly the situation at the time it was written.

It is always difficult to know where to begin, especially when one sits at a long porch table covered with papers, distracted by the beautiful, tree-fringed lake out beyond, birds singing, clouds floating, water lap-lapping, and all the rest.

I shuffled and reshuffled the papers, discarding more than half of them, my idea being that each paper should take a step further or elaborate a particular theme a bit more. Still, where to begin? Finally, I decided to begin with the two most recently written papers, not precisely because they were the most current of papers spreading over a decade or so, but because the first reveals me more clearly than the others. Somehow this sounds immodest, and I do not mean it in this sense. Rather, it seemed that anyone reading what I have to say about higher education in general and Catholic higher education in particular should have some idea of where I begin, what I think of my role as president of Notre Dame, what I perceive leadership to be. If I have no clear idea about *that*, then there is no profit in reading further. Everything I write begins with this vantage point, with a clear emphasis on values.

The second paper, the most recent of all, gives an overview of American higher education, where it has been and where it seems to be going. Again, this is the world I mainly inhabit and most of what I say pertains to the values that make this a very special world indeed.

In the various chapters that follow, I have tried to speak mainly in the second section to what has been the central endeavor of my life, the formation of a great Catholic university in modern America, and the problems and opportunities of Christian higher education generally. All American higher educational efforts, as universities worldwide historically, began with the churches. This is approached both comprehensively and in detail. I hope that one cannot read this first part without acquiring some sense of how I feel most deeply about the subject.

The third section is of broader scope because I am here mainly addressing myself to special problems in all of American higher education, again with special emphasis on values. It will be obvious to the reader that those broader concerns to which I was attracted and in which I became involved on the national or international scene, such as science and technology, human rights, human development, and values, began to loom larger in how I thought about higher education everywhere and anywhere, beyond the purely Catholic context.

The fourth section is a special approach to what has to have been the most interesting, difficult, and challenging period in my forty-four years as a student, professor, and administrator in higher education. Several times, at about two-year intervals, during the worldwide student revolution of the late sixties and early seventies, I had to pause and take stock, to try to understand what was happening and what we might learn from the experience. I believe that each time I learned a little more, and at the end was able to pull together the total experience. It also seemed appropriate to offer a case study that may be of historical importance should we ever face this kind of crisis again. It is easier to forget hard times, but wiser to learn from them.

Finally, in the concluding section, I try to take a look ahead at what the church, the university, and the world may become as we approach the new millennium, the year 2000. Here I try to capture the spirit of hope that is represented by the motto on the entrance to our National Archives in Washington: "What is past is prelude."

I should say in all honesty that it may be judged unwise to expose myself so personally in all that is written here, especially since the thoughts were prepared for living audiences, and still are in their original form, speaking directly to those audiences, who were wise or unwise in inviting me. Yet, this is what I mainly have said and still want to say, immodestly perhaps, about American higher education after spending my whole life in this endeavor. The recurrent theme of values is, I believe, needed today and might, I trust, be useful to a wider audience.

Throughout the book, I try to put each chapter in focus by giving a brief introduction. This was the most interesting part for me, since it brought back happy memories of times past. These brief vignettes will, I hope, also add a footnote to the educational history of our time, which, as I mention somewhere, call to mind Dickens's wonderful opening to *A Tale of Two Cities*, "It was the best of times; it was the worst of times." I suppose it can be called the worst because we went through the second great crisis in 341 years of American higher education. It was the best of times because we tripled in 20 years the results of more than three centuries of American effort in higher education, thereby hastening the crisis.

The most recurrent theme in all that is written here is the importance of values in higher education. I realize full well that education is essentially a work of the intellect, the formation of intelligence, the unending search for knowledge. Why then be concerned with values? Because wisdom is more than knowledge, man is more than his mind, and without values, man may be intelligent but less than fully human.

I enjoyed the effort of putting all of this together in some kind of coherent whole, perhaps more coherent to me than to the reader, since I was always in the middle of it, wondering, learning, growing I hope, suffering occasionally I am sure, but always grateful that of all the lives a priest might lead, this was certainly one of the most exciting, most enjoyable, and most rewarding. For all those who helped make it so, I would like to say at this time and in this place that I am most grateful to one and all of them.

Land O'Lakes, Wisconsin, June 1, 1978

SECTION ONE

An Overview

In 1976, I had a call from Roger Heyns, the president of the American Council on Education, the premier educational association in America, asking me to give the keynote address to the ACE's annual convention in New Orleans during October. Roger said that the meeting was going to be on educational leadership and that, since I had been around longer than most, he thought I should speak first. It was difficult to say no to Roger, since I had been on the search committee that selected him for president.

I said yes and then, as usual, worried about when I would get the ideas together, the talk written. I had another difficult task pending on a subject I knew less about—women's liberation and civil rights.

By pure chance, a trip I was to make in August was canceled, so I begot myself to Land O'Lakes, Wisconsin, where I have an easy claim on a cabin by the water.

I brought along a lot of books and articles about presidential leadership. Sitting by the fireside one night, contemplating all those books, I said to myself: "Ted, if you haven't learned a few things about presidential leadership in the past twenty-five years on the job, then you really are a monumental fraud. Put the books down and reflect. Then write and see what comes out." Well, this is what came out. I was worried that it might be a bit too personal, but I've had many calls from my colleagues, especially those new in a presidency, who said it helped. A week after the meeting in New Orleans, candidate Jimmy Carter was speaking at Notre Dame. I slipped him a copy, and he commented from it a few days later. In the hope that it might help others, here it is.

The University President

I have been asked to say something about presidential leadership in the field of higher education. In view of the fact that this is my twenty-fifth year as president of Notre Dame, I assume that I am expected to be somewhat personal, philosophical, frank, even blunt about the possibilities and challenges of being president.

First, let me abandon modesty by saying that the presidency of a college or university can be a great vocation: exciting, demanding, surprising, at times very satisfying, and occasionally great fun. Of course, it is also very hard work, tiring to the point of exhaustion, repetitive, very often exasperating, but never really hopeless or dull, if you have the right attitude about it.

I suppose one can say the same thing of the presidency of any human organization. All presidents, because they are at the top of whatever organizational triangle they are asked to lead, have broad and diverse constituencies, all clamoring for attention. The president often pleases one of his constituencies at the price of alienating another. To paraphrase Lincoln, you can please some of the constituencies all of the time, and all of the constituencies some of the time, but you cannot please all of your constituencies all of the time. I believe that a failure to recognize this basic fact, and a futile attempt to please everyone all of the time is the basic cause of most presidential failure. Clark Kerr, in his 1963 Godkin Lectures at

Harvard, best described the difficulty facing the president:

> The university president in the United States is expected to be a friend of the students, a colleague of the faculty, a good fellow with the alumni, a sound administrator with the trustees, a good speaker with the public, an astute bargainer with the foundations and the federal agencies, a politician with the state legislature, a friend of industry, labor, and agriculture, a persuasive diplomat with donors, a champion of education generally, a supporter of the professions (particularly law and medicine), a spokesman to the press, a scholar in his own right, a public servant at the state and national levels, a devotee of opera and football equally, a decent human being, a good husband and father, an active member of a church. Above all, he must enjoy traveling in airplanes, eating his meals in public, and attending public ceremonies. No one can be all of these things. Some succeed at being none.
>
> He should be firm, yet gentle; sensitive to others, insensitive to himself; look to the past and the future, yet be firmly planted in the present; both visionary and sound; affable, yet reflective; know the value of a dollar and realize that ideas cannot be bought; inspiring in his visions, yet cautious in what he does; a man of principle, yet able to make a deal; a man with broad perspective who will follow the details conscientiously; a good American, but ready to criticize the status quo fearlessly; a seeker of truth where the truth may not hurt too much; a source of public policy pronouncements when they do not reflect on his own institution. He should sound like a mouse at home and look like a lion abroad. He is one of the marginal men in a democratic society—of whom there are many others—on the margin of many groups, many ideas, many endeavors, many characteristics. He is a marginal man, but at the very center of the total process.

When my predecessor, Father John Cavanaugh, introduced me to the presidency, he gave me some very brief and very good advice that I will share with you today. May I say that I have tried to follow this advice, and following it has in large measure accounted for whatever sanity and equilibrium I still maintain after all these years.

First, Father John said, the heart of administration is making decisions. When you make a decision, however large or small, do not ask, "What is the easy thing to do?" or "What will cost the least money?" or "What will make me the most loved or popular by those affected by the decision?" Just ask what is the *right* decision, all things considered. Once you have made that judgment, and you'll make it better once you have been burned a few times, then just do it, decide it, no matter how difficult it is, no matter how costly, no matter how unpopular. In the long run, whatever the immediate uproar or inconveniences, people, your people, will respect you for following your conscience, for doing what you thought right, even though they do not agree with you. No other position is in the least way defensible, even in the short run. As Churchill once said so well: "The only guide to a man is his conscience. The only shield to his memory is the rectitude and sincerity of his actions. It is very imprudent to walk through life without this shield, because we are so often mocked by the failure of our hopes; but with this shield (of conscience) whatever our destiny may be, we always march in the ranks of honor." Martin Luther said the same thing more briefly, "Here I stand."

Every decision is not, of course, a great moral crisis. But I have found few decisions that did not have a moral dimension that could only be ignored with considerable risk, not just for oneself, but particularly for justice, whose final spokesmen all presidents are. When the president abdicates this fundamental responsibility, people are hurt.

One sees easily that what this attitude often calls for in the president is personal courage, often lonely courage, because everyone else below has passed the buck. If a person does not have the courage to stand alone, quite often, sometimes daily during times of crisis, then the presidency can be an agony. Without courage, it is always a failure. Of that I am sure.

The president's situation is unique. Politicians try to please everybody; presidents must please their conscience, ultimately God. Budget officers understandably try to find the most economical solution. It is not always the right one. Cowards, of course, seek the easy, undemanding path. Pasternak said in *Doctor Zhivago* that "gregariousness is the refuge of the mediocre." The uncertain always walk in a crowd. The leader most often finds himself marching single file at the head of a thin column. If you are to be a good president, you will often enough find yourself in that lonely situation, which brings me to the second Cavanaugh principle for the presidency.

"Don't expect a lot of praise or plaudits for what you do. If you need continual compliments to sustain you, you are in for a great surprise and letdown, because you are not going to get many thanks, even for the best things you do, the best decisions you make." Face it. People, as a group, are fickle, often insensitive, and the academic community is made up of people. As the congressman running for reelection was asked by a farmer he had helped greatly in the past, "What have you done for me lately, and what will you do for me tomorrow?"

In the last analysis, this second principle reverts to the first: you make a decision simply because it is right, in your judgment, not because someone will be grateful to you for making it. I grant you this is a difficult truism to accept because we are all human beings who enjoy an occasional pat on the back. I must assure you it is more realistic to expect numerous kicks in another part of your anatomy when you make a mistake. Criticism will be a far greater part of your presidential life than plaudits and gratitude. As John Cavanaugh said, you will sleep better if you recognize that from the beginning and don't court disappointment and personal hurt by expecting what you will not get.

One of the best early decisions I made elicited only one letter of thanks from the several hundred faculty who were greatly benefited by the decision. I thought it might get better as the years passed, but, believe me, it does not. Better to expect very little because that is what you will get in the way of praise or thanks. Once you accept this fact, then you can get on with doing what you do because it is the right thing to do. Besides, you get paid more than all the others and they may think that is thanks enough. Whether it is or not, it will have to do, so accept what is and don't be hurt.

The third bit of advice was very apropos because I was young and feisty at the time, also supremely confident as the young, thank God, always are. Cavanaugh Principle No. 3 was, "Don't think you can do very much all by yourself. There are too many of them and only one of you. Leadership may appear to be a man on a white horse leading the multitude, but you'll do a lot better if you get off the horse and entice the best of the multitude to join you up front." Of course, every leader has to have a personal vision of where he or she wants to lead, but just having it won't do it. Effective leadership means getting the best people you can find to share the vision and help in achieving it. Whether you are talking about being president of the United States or president of Willow Grove College, the principle is equally valid. You cannot do it alone, all by yourself. You may be very intelligent, exceptionally talented, good-looking, charismatic, whatever. You still need help, the very best help you can find. The third principle says: find them quickly and invite them aboard.

I remember, after hearing this, picking the five best people available and making them all vice-presidents. They were all older than I was. Some were more intelligent. They all possessed talents that I lacked. They often disagreed with me and often they were right, so I changed my mind. It was not always easy working with them, but it would have been impossible without them. They saved my life more times than I like to remember. My present associates are still saving my life today.

Cavanaugh added a few subthoughts to this third principle that one cannot be a good president all by himself or herself, making all the decisions unilaterally or intuitively, initiating everything all by oneself, always thinking and acting alone. Only God does that, and I believe even He is a trinity of persons.

Cavanaugh's three subthoughts were varied, but very valid in my later experience:

1. Don't think that you are the indispensable man (or woman). "The day you leave, someone else will be doing your

job," he said, "and quite probably doing it better." That rankled my pride, but I accepted it. I still do. Humility is not just a nice virtue; it is the truth. The cemeteries of the world are full of indispensable men and women, but somehow the world goes on. So does the world of colleges and universities.

2. Be sure that all those who help you achieve your vision receive a large share of the credit. It should not always be, "The president announces." Let a few others announce, too; especially, let them announce what they do successfully, and let them get what credit goes with it. Don't be afraid to be off center-stage once in a while. And while you may not get many thanks, make a point of seeing that all of those who work closely with you get thanked, at least by you. If there is any long-range credit for what is well done in your institution, you will eventually get your share, maybe at their expense, so make sure that they get a good word of gratitude from you right now.

3. Never pass off on your associates all the dirty work of administration. Never let them pass their less tasty tasks to you either. As a general rule, you will and should take the blame in public for the large mistakes that would not have happened if you had been better informed, more involved, even more decisive. On the other hand, don't baby your associates when they tend to hide behind you, or get you to do what they find unpleasant. Tell them that you will handle your own unpleasant duties and that they will handle theirs. I once had a doorman who couldn't bring himself to tell people not to park in front of the university inn, where there was a large No Parking sign. After I chided him, his way out was to say to all comers, "Father Hesburgh doesn't want you to park here." After I heard of this, I said to him, "I'll make a deal with you. I won't interfere with the parking, if you don't use me to do it right."

The fourth principle was not spoken as much as lived by my predecessor. When an author in Renaissance Italy, around the time of Machiavelli, wanted to write about the science of governance, he asked the best governor he knew, the duke of Mantua, what was the most important quality of the person who governs well. The duke quickly answered in two words:

essere umano, to be human.

That may seem to be an oversimplification at first glance. After thinking about it, in the light of much experience, I would say that it strikes to the heart of what a good president should be, simply human. Those presidents who are generally unsuccessful fail often from lack of humanity. They lose the loyalty of those with whom they live and work. All our dealings are with people, all kinds of people: people who are intelligent and not so intelligent; people who are good or bad, but generally a mixture of both; people who have hopes, dreams, feelings, frustrations; people who are happy or unhappy; people who are satisfied or dissatisfied; people who generally want something that we can or cannot give. All of them deserve something from us that we can give, no matter what the outcome of our decisions, namely to be treated as human beings, to be understood, even when that is difficult, to be accorded basic human consideration and compassion, even when they abuse our human dignity. In a word, people deserve to be treated with humane sensitivity, even when all our inclinations push us towards brusque rejection, not only of their proposals, but also of themselves, as persons. The president has to suffer fools, if not gladly, at least patiently.

Animals govern by growling or biting; human dictators rule by sheer force, terror, or quick punishment, even death. That is not what is or should be expected in a community of learners and teachers who have long been characterized by rationality, civility, urbanity, friendship, but especially, humanity towards one another, even when they are intellectually or morally in disagreement.

There is a humane way of saying no, of denying an impassioned request, of telling someone that he or she has failed and will be terminated. There is a humane way of upholding a deeply held conviction, even when it is under brutal attack. One can be forceful and humane at the same time. But it is not easy.

It may be that the most difficult problem for a president is to be humane while doing many unpleasant but necessary things that seem to others to be inhumane. *Essere umano*, to be human, a great quality in anyone having power over others.

Power will not corrupt such a person.

I would now like to declare myself on some very specific opportunities and challenges that face every college or university president. The easiest way to do so is to discuss in some detail the relationships between the president and his central constituencies: the trustees, the faculty, the students. You have all heard the facetious comment that a successful president gives each group what it wants: the alumni—championship teams; the faculty—parking; and the students—sex. I find this cynical, as well as bad policy.

The trustees are in a juridical sense the most important constituency since they have, in our American structure for higher education, the very important task of setting basic policies for the administration of what is essentially a public trust. The trustees do not administer the institution, but their most important task is to see that it is well administered. Having selected and appointed the president, the least they should expect of him is honesty and clarity of purpose, even when the trustees may not agree. Disagreement there often may be between a president and his trustees, but never deceit.

There are times when a president will have to try to change trustees' minds regarding basic policy. At least he should leave no doubt about where he stands. Trustees often need to be informed clearly and forcefully, on a continuing basis, regarding the institution's most basic needs. The president must resist when trustees interfere in the administration, attempting to govern rather than insure good government. I have found that this stance is both appreciated and supported by trustees. A spirit of confidence on the part of a president begets confidence on the part of trustees.

Trustees should share bad as well as good news, problems as well as successes. Sometimes a president should simply admit that he or she has made a mistake. Most of the trustees I know do not expect perfection of a president, just competent effort and honest accounting of stewardship. In occasional times of great crisis, trustees must be reminded by a president that they are the court of last resort, that they must take a corporate stand, that no one is going to follow the sound of an uncertain trumpet.

There may even come a time when the president must say to the trustees, because only he or she can, "Here I stand." It may be the end of the relationship, but rarely is. Even trustees, or maybe especially trustees, respect integrity.

All in all, this has not been in my experience a difficult relationship, even though the president is always in the middle, between the trustees and the rest of the institution. He must interpret both sides to each other, preserving the confidence of each side. I should admit that I have always been blessed by intelligent and competent trustees, well versed in the problems of higher education. Had it been otherwise, I might be telling a different story, although I believe my principles of operation would be the same.

The faculty are, from an educational point of view, the most important constituency of the president. Educationally, the faculty make the institution what it is, good or bad or in between. The faculty are also the president's most difficult constituency. He is their leader, but the trustees appoint him. Every day of every year, year in and year out, the president must prove himself to the faculty. Especially in a large institution, there is no such thing as a completely cordial and trusting relationship. The president is, in some sense, the symbolic adversary, since he is ultimately the bearer of whatever bad news come to the faculty these days.

On the positive side, and more importantly, he must proclaim to them, in season and out, his vision of their institution, what it is and what it might yet be. Only they can make his dream come true, and only if they are convinced will they cooperate in the venture. In a word, he must create trust, no easy task, given the climate.

There is no leadership here by edict. All faculty consider themselves his equal, if not his better, intellectually. Persuasion is the best mode of leadership where the faculty are involved. They must be part and parcel of the total educational process.

There are no easy answers here. Most presidents have been members of a teaching and research faculty and thus are fully conscious of the hopes and aspirations, as well as the very special nature, of that body called faculty, made up of people who think otherwise.

And yet, they too must be led by the president. He must find a theme of unity in their diversity. He must inspire them, challenge them, question them, reason with them, occasionally say no to them; but, above all, he must persuade them to give their best talents and their most creative efforts to the realization of his educational vision.

This assumes, of course, that the president does have a clear vision for the institution, a vision that is educationally sound and integral, given the available resources. You cannot turn Pugwash into Princeton overnight. Whatever else he is clear and enthusiastic about, the president must most of all elaborate his specific vision, rethink it as times change, perfect it as he learns from experience or develops new resources. He may be the best administrator in the world, but without a clear and bright and, yes, beautiful vision, he is leading nowhere. Without a vision, the people perish. Each president will have his own style, no matter, but beyond all style must be substance. If a president cannot intelligently discuss education with his faculty, nothing else he discusses will matter. He will simply lose the faculty and he will be unable to lead them anywhere, certainly not to the promised land.

The normal faculty criticisms of a president are many and varied, often contradictory. If he is always home, he is a nobody; if he is often away, he is neglecting his homework. If he spends little time with faculty, he is aloof; if he spends much time with them, he is interfering in their proper business. If he balances the budget, he is stingy; if he cannot balance the budget, he is irresponsible and incompetent. If he is big on fringe and retirement benefits, the younger faculty can't meet their expenses; if he stresses faculty raises, the older faculty are impoverished on retirement. If he spends much time on fund raising, he is a huckster; if he doesn't, the financial situation gets worse. In a word, it is Scylla and Charybdis every day. We might as well admit that willy-nilly, the president will always be between the rock and the hard place.

Having admitted this, let us also admit that there is no better association in the world than a good academic relationship where civility rules disagreement—and comradeship is very real in an endeavor as fundamentally exalted as higher education. Despite all the normal and natural tensions between good faculty and good administration, this is in itself a healthy tension productive of an unusually good symbiotic effect—better governance by mutual understanding of the tasks proper to each.

I could understate the situation by saying that administrators should mainly administer and professors should mainly teach. When either intrudes unnecessarily upon the other's task, both tasks are unduly complicated and rendered impossible. There are many other schemes of governance discussed widely and promoted actively today. In fact, sandbagging the administration by a constant threat of collective bargaining has become a popular indoor sport in colleges and universities. Despite this, I have yet to hear of any form of governance as good as what we generally have, especially when intelligently and competently administered, with the faculty deeply involved in the formation of educational policy and the administration sensitively and forcefully administering this policy, even prodding occasionally for a change of policy. Both functions are indispensable: the forming and the effecting of educational policy mutually agreed upon. There are, of course, many other tasks that faculty and administration must do separately. Here, mutual understanding and cooperation are the order of the good day in academe.

Having already specified two constituencies as most important, I won't surprise you by declaring that the students, as the main reason for which our institutions exist, are also, in that sense, a most important constituency of the president. Their needs and desires do not always coincide with those of the trustees and faculty, but they, too, must be heard. Let us admit that it took a recent student revolution for us to involve them more integrally in the total life of our institutions. Personally, I believe that the students have generally reacted well to this new responsibility, as new members of most of our academic councils and committees.

The greatest gift a president can give his students is the example of his life. One could say the same of faculty, but the president is in a highly visible position. He must be a kind of super professor to all the students. Young adults are, whether they admit it or not, looking for public models of the kind of person they would like to become. While the president cannot be a super *"in loco parentis* person," he cannot avoid transmitting to students the fact that he does or does not care deeply about the kinds of persons they are becoming, the interests and attitudes they presently portray, the concerns that bite deeply into their youthful hopes.

Despite anything he says, the president will declare much more by how he lives, the concerns he exemplifies, the causes he supports, the public service he renders. There are great moral issues facing young and old alike today. In an educational setting, one would hope that values would be all important and that the young would perceive clearly where we elders stand on issues like human rights, world poverty and hunger, good government, preserving the fragile ecosphere, strengthening marriage and family life, to mention a few issues.

The president should also be deeply concerned that his students are being educated for tomorrow, not for yesterday; that they do emerge from the whole process knowing how to think, write, speak, and organize themselves effectively; that they have a sense of values and judge their world by reason and justice with love and not by blind emotional instinct; finally, that they have situated themselves and are at peace with themselves as they are and are becoming, as men and women, as Protestants, Catholics, or Jews, as members of a Western world that is part of a much poorer, less humane, underdeveloped, and increasingly interdependent world. One would hope that beyond competence in doing something to earn a living, students would emerge from our institutions with some compassion for and commitment to the improvement of the larger, less-favored world around them. If we, as presidents, do not show these concerns in our own lives and works, then I doubt that our students will take any of our words very seriously.

Each president will have to find some realistic and personal way of maintaining a continuing conversation with his students, not only for their benefit, but also mainly for his own. Students will keep a president alive and honest for they have an extraordinary radar for detecting double talk and the irrelevant. One must always level with them.

Again, I believe that under the pressure of the student revolution, there were too many concessions made to the bohemian type of students. It is time and overtime to revert to a student way of life that is more wholesome and less unstructured. I know of no way of building character without adhering to a definite set of moral standards and values that make for the good life. We have cast aside too many of these standards and values, like honesty, sobriety, fidelity, justice, and magnanimity. I believe many students, quite different from those of the late sixties, would welcome a change, a reestablishment of student standards. Change will not come without presidential leadership.

I could, but will not, speak at length of other constituencies of the president: the alumni, who are the best evidence of our productive and continuing efforts; the public, who largely gave birth to our institutions and generously support them when we win their appreciation of our work. Both are important. I could also speak of the government, local, state, and federal, that today has such impact, maybe too much, on our institutions. However, I have said enough in these personal reflections on the presidency.

I will only say that I am concerned that so many recently appointed presidents are fleeing a task that could be very fulfilling and greatly productive if approached with vision, hope, and reasonable confidence. I have seen the presidency in its best and worst days. I did not enjoy the troubled times—of student unrest or of financial exigency—but the good years before and since have more than compensated for them. I only regret that we lost so many good and stalwart presidents who were caught in a vortex for which there were no set rules of procedure, only improvisations, many of which simply did not work. Higher education must still produce a whole new generation of presidents who are their equals. It was a sad commentary that when *Change* magazine identified by popular poll last year the forty leaders of higher education, so very few of them were presidents of colleges and universities, and of the top four, only one.

I would like to close on a very personal note, which I trust you will indulge me. Over the years, I have stood at the graveside of many of my university colleagues and have contemplated the quiet nobility of their lives, so totally and unselfishly given to the higher education of young men and women. Some day, some of my lifelong associates will stand at my graveside. At that time, I would be greatly honored if they should say, "Well, we worked together for a long time. We didn't always agree, but that never bothered our friendship or our forward march. At least, he was fair and tried to make the place better. Now he can rest in peace."

I'm not anxious for that day to come soon, but when it does, I would settle for those final sentiments. Who among us would ask for more? The respect of our colleagues is quite enough, assuming God's blessing, too. We won't get the one without the other.

In a world that is largely divided, one of the greatest assets of higher education is that those who lead the total worldwide endeavor do stand together, sharing their challenges and opportunities. This is done largely through the International Association of Universities, based in Paris and attached to UNESCO.

We meet every five years—the last time in Moscow. At each quinquennial meeting, we elect a council representing all the universities of the world. In Moscow, we elected Martin Meyerson, president of the University of Pennsylvania, to represent the universities of the United States.

In the spring of 1978, I had a call from Marty saying that the council of the IAU was having its meeting this year in the United States at the University of Pennsylvania in Philadelphia. He asked that I come and give the main address on the past and present of American higher education, with some indication of our future problems.

I mentioned that the date he indicated was a bad one for me, since I was chairing the annual meeting of the board of the Rockefeller Foundation in New York City that day. He had done his homework and said he understood that we would be finished by five o'clock. If I would hurry over to the heliport at Sixtieth Street on the East River, he would have a helicopter there to take me directly to Philadelphia, where we would land on the roof of a building adjacent to the University. Their dinner would begin at seven, which would give ample time for me to arrive and deliver the address.

This chapter was mostly written on airplanes between Chicago and the West Coast on two successive trips there. Maybe this gives some indication of the fact that the halcyon days of the ivory-tower university life have changed, and this, indeed, may be one of the problems not mentioned in the address.

As you will note, I am especially indebted to Lord Eric Ashby, former vice-chancellor of Cambridge University, whose understanding of university life in England, America, Africa, and Asia is phenomenal. More than that, his constant theme of the necessity of excellence as the hallmark of higher education everywhere is a constant inspiration and ideal to all of us.

There may be other important challenges beyond those mentioned in the address, but I believe that for America and the world, the problems I mention are very real and very urgent in our day. How we cope with them will spell success or failure for higher education everywhere in the years ahead.

I can only speak for America. In this, I am optimistic in saying that we will face the challenge and add a new chapter to the worldwide history of higher education by becoming ever more open and ever more excellent, less politicized and more academic, increasing our inherent freedom while exercising it more responsibly. If I am correct in prognosticating this, we will indeed become a model for all the world as universities that provide both the ideas and the human leadership that validate our always precarious existence.

II

The Past and Present of American Higher Education

You have all heard the French saying that is a tribute to the ancient Greek cyclical theory of history: "Plus ça change, plus c'est la même chose"—the more things change, the more they are the same. I am not sure that this is so, if one views the history of higher education in America, which begins with Harvard College in 1636. There certainly has been a great deal of change, but I am not sure we are back to where we began, unless one considers as very important a vestigial yearning today for structure, tradition, and values as central to the educational process.

American higher education began in order to educate gentlemen and professionals—first ministers of religion, but soon enough, lawyers and doctors and teachers as well. In this it was not unlike the early medieval universities, where theology, law, medicine, and professing were central.

In the earliest of American colleges, classical languages, Latin, Greek, and Hebrew, and classical literature and history, including, of course, the Bible, were most important. This continued to be true for over two-hundred years.

The first great departure came during the Civil War, in 1863, when Lincoln signed the Morrill Act inaugurating the land-grant universities in each of the states. The resulting agricultural and mechanical arts colleges were a far cry from the Ivy League classical ideal, but were, in fact, just what the growing nation needed as it moved into the great agricultural lands of the Midwest and West and into the industrial revolution as well. This development also represented a shift from private to public education, a first chapter in a transition from a totally private to a majority public system which ultimately came to pass after World War II, at which time we were about half public and half private. The land-grant act also represents the beginning of a populist trend in higher education in America, embryonic, but a beginning that would come to full fruition in the next century. The land-grant movement is perhaps the most significant innovation since universities began in medieval times. It was at the heart of American university development.

There was another almost parallel development that greatly influenced the course of American higher education. For the first two-and-a-half centuries of its history, teaching was a central, practically unique, concern, as was true in the Oxford-Cambridge prototypes which were our models. Then came the new German university emphasis on research and graduate studies, which entered the American scene a century ago with the founding of specifically research and graduate universities such as Johns Hopkins. A symbiosis soon enough took place. The other great existing universities began to emphasize research and graduate studies while the newly founded research universities also began accepting undergraduates.

In time, particularly since World War II, all of these influences merged as might be expected. Many of our older universities, once classical colleges, and many of our land-grant universities, once called cow colleges, became indistinguishable in their aims as great teaching and research institutions. There were peripheral differences, of course. The Harvards, Yales, Princetons, Chicagos, Stanfords were still private institutions with smaller and, therefore, more highly selective student bodies, but they are challenged in almost every university aspect by the Michigans, Wisconsins, and Berkeleys. Among the more than three thousand institutions of higher education here, there are, at least in my judgment, about a hundred great universities in America today, of which half would be private and half public—although three-quarters of all the students in higher education would be in public institutions, which are less numerous but generally larger than private institutions of higher learning. The greatest growth in higher education since World War II has been in community colleges, public institutions catering to masses of urban students who can live at home while attending these nearby colleges.

Following World War II, there was a third emphasis or purpose introduced into universities in America, namely service to the local community, the state, the nation, and the world. If it were possible at that time, they would have included service to the solar system and the universe. After all, we are universities and this was a period of unmatched optimism and growth. The service involved just about everything that faculty and students could do, and some things as well that they could not do. It was all very well intentioned, and it did seem to reemphasize the importance of the university to the society at large that supports it—but in my present judgment, service loomed too large and promised much that it could not deliver. Service functions distracted many faculty and some students from research and teaching and learning, which are certainly more central to the role of the university.

When the student revolution came in the sixties, we who were about to reform and recreate the world found that we often could not control our own central campuses and those who were violently disrupting them. From being enormously outward looking, we suddenly reversed our attentions and became inward looking, reassessing what we were doing and becoming a good deal less service-oriented and less outwardly directed in the process. We are still involved in service to society, but each new project is much more closely scrutinized and more realistically appraised in view of its contribution or noncontribution to the central purposes of the university—to teach, to learn, to research, to educate.

I have indulged in this rather kaleidoscopic and broad-brush review of the course of higher learning in America so that the comments I make about the present and future of American higher education might be seen better in the perspective of what has been, in the historical context. We live in a day when where we have been does not seem quite as important as where we are and where we are going. Happily, this ahistorical or antihistorical attitude is beginning to change. Note the popularity of Alex Haley's book, *Roots*. In my judgment, we cannot understand why or where we are without looking at where we came from and why. As to the future, we either understand the lessons of the past and learn from them or we do indeed repeat, as Santayana warned, all our past mistakes, which were numerous by anybody's count.

Where are we going in higher education in America today? May I suggest several themes that I confess to be my personal opinion and not necessarily agreed to by my American colleagues.

Christian theologians generally think in trilogies and, since I began my university life as a Christian theologian, I trust you will forgive me if I discuss three modern trends or central concerns in American higher education. My three themes, questions, concerns, or problems, if you wish, are these:

1. *Whom* should we be teaching in higher education? Many students or few, elitist or populist choices, majorities or minorities? In a word, this is a problem of access. Related directly to this problem is the effect our decision will have on the work of higher education, basically the problem of trying to achieve quality and equality at the same time.

2. *What* should we teach? This is a problem of curriculum, of substance, of degrees granted, and basic cores of education.

3. *How* should we manage the whole endeavor? This is a problem of governance which is not unrelated to financing, autonomy, and academic freedom. These are perennial university problems.

The first problem is one of quality and equality. Since the problem only involves one letter of the alphabet, I am reminded of the violent quarrels between fourth-century theologians regarding two key Greek words, similarly different by only one letter—*homoousios* and *homoiousios*. I think the theologians' problem was more fundamental than ours—

theological problems *are* generally more fundamental than social problems—but our problem is really at the heart of American society, as well as central to American educational policy today.

America was born with the wonderful statement of the Declaration of Independence, "We hold these truths to be self-evident, that all men are created equal. . . ." That was indeed, in 1776, a philosophical mouthful. It took us the better part of two centuries to make it come true for most Americans, women as well as men, black as well as white, young as well as old, poor as well as rich. We are still making history, but I do believe that the fundamental struggle for equality has been largely won. I say largely because there is still a distance to go. Even saying largely cannot deny that.

Now I would like to put the case of quality versus equality in its most recent lineaments in the modern history of higher education. Because America was grateful to those who risked their lives for world freedom in World War II, higher education was opened and subsidized, as never before, for millions of returning veterans. We called this legislation the GI Bill. The result was perhaps the best investment that our government ever made. By 1950, there were 3 million in colleges and universities. Once the floodgates were opened and aspirations raised, the movement was only in one direction—upward. As a young instructor, teaching these veterans and being their chaplain in the years following 1945, I can personally attest that they brought a new spirit, a new enthusiasm for upward mobility to higher education. They were great—and their achievement spelled equality—or access—as never before. A whole new day had dawned, and the light would be three times brighter in the next twenty years—almost four times, if you extrapolate it to our day: 3 to 11 million students in higher education.

Then in 1957, something else happened. It was called Sputnik. All of a sudden, this vaunted higher education in America seemed second-rate. This was, in fact, a bad conclusion from dramatic, though inconclusive, evidence, but there it was. Immediately, the emphasis was laid on for quality. We had to be the best. At the time, I was a member of a key governmental body, the National Science Board. When I joined the board in 1954, we had a budget of $6 million for basic research, mainly in universities. When I finished my twelve-year term in 1966, the National Science Foundation budget had grown to $600 million. That says something about the thrust for quality in higher education—the main target of our NSF funds. This period might be called the decade of quality because this was our main concern.

Then in the middle sixties, we had a concurrent revolution for equality. I was part of that, too, and no less enthusiastically, as a member and later chairman of the United States Commission on Civil Rights. We broke all the barriers, educational and otherwise, for blacks and other minorities in the mid-sixties. We often conveniently forget that prior to the middle sixties, we had an all-pervasive system of apartheid in all our thirteen Southern states, almost as bad as South Africa's today. All this apartheid was eliminated, as a system, almost overnight, by the federal civil rights laws of 1964, 1965, and 1967.

The new equality for minorities, particularly blacks, was dramatically evident in education. The *de jure* segregated elementary and secondary school system in the South was largely eliminated within a five-year period. All the great universities in the land, North and South, so enlarged their black enrollments through affirmative action and new scholarship programs that within a decade the proportion of black high school graduates enrolling in colleges and universities was equal to that of whites. Blacks, who numbered only about two hundred in what were predominantly white medical schools, North and South, ten years ago, now have over three thousand enrolled. As the Bakke case testifies, there is a new concern today, the very opposite of that a decade ago, namely, reverse discrimination in favor of minorities. Parenthetically, my personal opinion on this point is that we arrived at the past condition of unjust disequilibrium between the numbers of black and white university graduates and professional persons because of an age-old practice of unjust discrimination against blacks and other minorities. It will take a *temporary* reverse discrimination, or affirmative action, to balance the scales of justice, meeting the promise of our Constitution regarding the equality of all Americans. Constitutional law as invoked in the Bakke case should not be used to thwart the most basic concern of the Constitution: equal justice for all.

This then is, in brief compass, the recent history of our striving for quality and equality in American higher education. What then is the problem? Basically, the problem is that we need in American higher education both quality and equality. That was the title of the first report of the Carnegie Commission on Higher Education, published in 1968. However, I believe that given the enormous influence of federally financed programs on higher education, we have gone from a massive financing of quality following Sputnik to a much more massive financing of equality or access to higher education following the civil rights revolution of the middle sixties. It was calculated last year that the federal government was then spending six times more for equality in higher education than for quality. The latest massive addition of $1.5 billion to the higher education budget announced by President Carter last February was totally in the area of equality, not quality.

A famous American comedian who died last year, Groucho Marx, used to jest: "Any club that will allow me to be a member isn't worth joining." Like all humor, there is a large grain of truth in this. Unless the quality of American higher education is kept on a high level and constantly improved—a very costly project—millions more will have access to that which is not all that much worth having if its value has become debased, its promise emptied.

Eric Ashby has put the case best in a 1970 essay, *Any Person, Any Study*: "In America the thin stream of intellectual excellence is kept clear by two intellectual devices: the highly selective university and the prestige of graduate school. No one, however dedicated to egalitarianism, is likely to advocate open admissions to the undergraduate college of Harvard or to graduate study in physics at Berkeley. But are these filters for excellence satisfactory? I venture to say no, they are not.

"There must be, within any system of education beyond high school, opportunities for the critical faculty to be sharpened to the point where it can challenge assumptions. This cannot be done except by close contact with men who really are intellectual masters. Not many students are fit for this discipline, but those who are must be able to find it, or the thin stream of intellectual excellence on which society depends for innovation, for wise judgment in unforeseen crises, for management of highly complex systems, will dry up."

I must insist again that all of this is costly, but without such quality education, at least in a significant number of institutions, the whole endeavor lapses into meaningless mediocrity. Later in the same essay, Ashby makes the same point with unusual clarity and forceful eloquence:

"All civilized countries depend upon a thin clear stream of excellence to provide new ideas, new techniques, and the statesmanlike treatment of complex social and political problems. Without the renewal of this excellence, a nation can drop to mediocrity in a generation. The renewal of excellence is expensive: the highly gifted student needs informal instruction, intimate contact with other first-class minds, opportunities to learn the discipline of dissent from men who have themselves changed patterns of thought; in a word (it is one which has become a five-letter word of reproach) this sort of student needs to be treated as *elite*. De Tocqueville long ago predicted that this would be anathema in an egalitarian society. He was right: by a curious twist of reasoning, persons who enthusiastically agree to supernormal educational expenditure on the intellectually underprivileged, oppose supernormal expenditure on the intellectually overprivileged, who need it just as much. It is commonly assumed that America has to choose between one or other of two patterns of higher education: mass or elite. I would deny this assumption. It is America's prime educational challenge to devise a coexistence of both patterns. There is already sufficient evidence to demonstrate that this could be done without dissolving and redesigning the whole system."

However optimistic one is about the possibilities of pursuing at the same time both quality and equality in higher education, I must say that we must achieve both simultaneously if the great enterprise that is America is to continue and to prosper and to realize its deepest human dreams. We educators must remove the stigma from the word "elite." When I am sick, I want an elite doctor, when on an airplane, an elite pilot, when in difficulty with the law, an elite lawyer. Who does not want elite doctors, elite lawyers, elite teachers, elite artists, elite scientists, elite engineers, elite architects? And where will they come from if not from elite education, open to the highest talent of every nation and race? There is a difference between equality and egalitarianism and there is a bottomless gulf between quality and mediocrity. I would hope that in the future, American higher education can always reflect both quality and equality rather than settle for being egalitarian and mediocre.

The second central problem facing us in American higher education today regards not who is taught and how they are taught, but rather what is taught. This problem basically concerns what it is to be educated, what common core of knowledge is essential to anyone claiming to be human and civilized. Put differently, is there any set of concepts, ideas, ideals, aspirations, hopes, and even dreams that can form a matrix within which human beings anywhere and everywhere can hold a meaningful discussion and discourse upon essential human concerns?

As indicated earlier in the brief historical sketch with which I began this chapter, there was a day several centuries ago, in a prescientific, preindustrial, colonial time when we thought we knew the common theme which gave a unity to education and a curriculum common to all universities. It is difficult to imagine, much less portray, what has happened to American higher education from the day 342 years ago when the first Harvard students, all nine of them, took about ten courses in classical languages, literature, and the Bible, all taught by the president. Today about 11 million students in America take over 2 million classes in about three thousand institutions, taught by a half-million faculty members. In contrast to that first Harvard degree, today there are over fifteen hundred separate degrees granted. Is any unity of language, knowledge, or discourse possible amid such modern diversity?

In some ways it is easier to understand and state the forces contrary to any curricular unity. A recent Carnegie publication, *Missions of the College Curriculum*, explains the problem of formulating a meaningful curriculum for higher education: "There are eternal points of tension: scholarship versus training; attention more to the past or to the present or to the future; integration versus fragmentation; socialization into the culture versus alienation from the culture; student choices versus institutional requirements; breadth versus depth; skills versus understanding versus personal interests; theory versus practice; ethical commitment versus ethical neutrality."

The first great departure from the unified curriculum of the first two centuries of American higher education came after our Civil War, with the advent of the land-grant colleges and the vast expansion of knowledge that led to specialization, different functional colleges and professional schools, especially departments catering to special careers and the specialized knowledge and research they required.

The second broad departure from an earlier unified curriculum came and is coming during the sixties and current seventies. As students become scarcer, and higher education approaches a steady-state condition, there is more of a consumer or market-oriented curriculum which seeks to attract unusual students, part-time and adult.

If one could oversimplify these three stages, the earlier curricular approach was cultural, the heritage of Western civilization, while the second was oriented towards knowledge for use or employment or industrial and rural development (the original land-grant ideal). The developing curriculum of today, while influenced by these earlier stages, is more geared to what seems relevant, allowing students to pick and choose among a wide range of so-called practical or artistic courses, many of which would formerly have been shunned like the plague in most institutions of higher education. Today such courses are the bread-and-butter attractions of many community colleges. In this recent endeavor, America is largely on its own, no longer emulating British or German university models.

In the face of these curricular developments, it is interesting to see how the undergraduates now choose their fields of study.

58 percent are in professional studies, including the widest range of occupational choices;

15 percent are majoring in the physical and natural sciences, especially biology;

8 percent in the social sciences;

6 percent in the arts;

5 percent in the humanities and 8 percent undistributed.

Looked at horizontally, despite these vertical choices of students, the various curricula generally include an almost equal remnant of the historical stages: one-third general or liberal courses; one-third specialized or major courses; and finally, a third part of elective courses, chosen at will and often at random. Restated somewhat cynically, one might say that students today are studying what the educators think they need to be minimally cultured, what the professionals think they need to be minimally competent to perform professionally, and lastly, what the students think they need and want to study, for a wide variety of motives.

One can say at least that all of this development leaves American higher education today enormously diverse and, depending on the exellence of the faculty and students and institutional requirements, widely varying in quality.

My personal response to the current situation is that especially we in select private and public research and teaching universities must ask ourselves what we are really trying to do through education and how realistically we are achieving our mission and goals through the present curriculum, which has evolved in response to myriad internal and external pressures.

I suggest that we give major attention to the humanistic or liberal aspects of the total course of studies, for it is only here that a student learns to situate himself or herself personally in a rapidly changing world, as a man or woman, as a religious or nonreligious person, as a member of a given race, nationality, culture, or tradition. It is mainly through liberal education that one learns how to think clearly, logically, beautifully; how to express oneself; how to learn continually in a wide variety of ways; how to evaluate ideas and ideals; how to appreciate where humankind has been and is going. Whatever else we do to educate our students, all these liberating qualities, skills, and concepts are essential to what kind of persons they are becoming, no matter what they are preparing to do in life. It is also, I believe, in this humanistic area that any curriculum will achieve a measure of unity and coherence. American higher education is ripe for an intellectual attempt at synthesis following a fairly long period of disintegrating and fragmenting specialization in all of the various disciplines. We should not expect our students to effect an integration of the knowledge we give them if we ourselves cannot plan or explain or understand that integration, or unity, or synthesis. If the curriculum explains best where we are and what we are doing as educators, then it deserves much more attention from presidents, deans, and faculties than it is receiving today.

The third and final concern or problem I would like to discuss briefly is university governance, how we manage the whole endeavor of American higher education.

Governance is in many ways a reflection of the educational history and ideals of this country. Since all of higher education was private and independent during the first few centuries, it is understandable that public education today is largely governed in the same tradition as the private sector, which borrowed from the British. We all have trustees as the highest governing body, a group generally chosen from the public at large. Then there is an academic senate or council, an internal body largely made up of faculty and administrators who control the internal academic decisions of the university, subject to trustee approval. Below the academic senate, there are a wide variety of collegiate, departmental, and student councils and committees, plus a large administrative body of president and chancellor at times, provost, vice-presidents, and deans.

We in America are more highly and more professionally organized than most European universities. I remember visiting Sir Maurice Bowra when he was vice-chancellor, chief executive officer, at Oxford University. At ten in the morning, he was sitting at an absolutely clean desk, not a paper, not a telephone, not a secretary in sight, reading a Greek book. "How does this place get run?" I asked, with some envy. "By tradition," he replied.

With all this organization which characterizes the governance of American higher education, how can there be a problem and a concern? May I say that governance of universities, everywhere in the world, will always have a problem in maintaining those two university characteristics which are ever difficult to uphold: autonomy and academic freedom.

The university is the only institution in modern society that is largely supported by society and yet claims a unique autonomy to criticize the very society that once gave it birth and now gives it financial support. There will always be governments and other university sponsors, such as churches and corporations, who will gag on this demand of autonomy. Yet, I would have to say quite proudly that in America, those who govern universities have managed in a superlative way to maintain the university's autonomy against all external and internal threats to the essential independence of the university community.

As the universities, even the private ones, depend more and more upon the federal and state governments for support, there will, I think, be increasing occasions for us to resist the bureaucratic urge to interfere with the university's essential independence, the move to insist that we do this or that or forfeit the beneficence of the state. We must be morally responsible in our exercise of autonomy, but within this moral parameter, we must be ever ready to say: take your support; we would rather have our freedom. This is always easier for private universities, who have other means of support, and this is one of the best reasons to maintain a balance of distinguished private as well as public universities in this land. In a very real way, our inherent independence and autonomy as private universities guarantees the same for the public universities.

Those who govern must also preserve the academic freedom of the university. The most obvious modern threat to this academic freedom is the modern move to politicize the university. This threat grew out of the student rebellion of the late sixties and early seventies. Fortunately, most American universities did not allow themselves to be politicized by the more radical elements of the faculty and students. Unfortunately, some European universities did overreact, and we are now paying the price for the reorganization that grew out of the demand for student participation in governance.

I recently learned of a very distinguished European university that will not be distinguished much longer because now it is largely governed by radical students and nonacademic staff who form the majority of most university councils. Faculty are now appointed and granted tenure not for their academic excellence, but for their ideological orthodoxy, according to the students' radical views. Thus is the university politicized, and in a politicized university, academic freedom becomes a travesty. In this once great university, standards have been lowered, the century-old university values regarding academic excellence have been bastardized, and all of the best faculty are leaving for freer lands. This is the tragedy that strikes when academic freedom dies.

Recently a law faculty member petitioned the governing board of his institution to declare a stand against abortion. He insisted that if his university could take a position on the Bakke case, it could do so on abortion, too.

He was opposed on the grounds that while Bakke is part of a university's concern about equal access to university professional schools, abortion is not directly related to higher educational concerns. To become involved in and to take an institutional position on every modern moral concern would ultimately destroy the university's freedom to do objectively and freely that which it does best. Again Lord Ashby has a word of wisdom: "The universities will have to reach a consensus about the limits of their responsibilities. A hospital is not expected to make corporate statements about political or social issues unless they impinge on the health service. Similarly a university's authority is preserved only if it remains corporately silent except on issues which impinge on education. Some of the dissent in universities today is due to a misinterpretation of this restraint. Because a hospital, a college, a museum, a library, do not corporately condemn war, it is not to be assumed that they corporately condone war. It is not commonly understood that institutional silence is necessary in order to safeguard freedom of speech among members of the institution. Instead, this silence in the academic community is taken, especially by the young, as evidence that intellectual detachment and the life of reason are inconsistent with social concern and emotional commitment. If universities and colleges are to survive as we know them, this illusion must be dispelled."

I must now conclude, and wish to do so by saying that as one who has spent the totality of his adult life, since age seventeen, in a university, I am happy to testify that there is no place where I would, upon serious reflection, rather live. A university is a wonderful home if one wishes to be intellectually alive, free, and ever open to further growth in mind and spirit.

SECTION TWO

The Contemporary Catholic
and
Christian University

We had no centenary celebration at Notre Dame in 1942 because the whole world was at war and we were at that time a vast training camp for naval officers, some 25,000 of whom passed through, mainly as ninety-day wonders. When 1967 arrived, someone had the bright idea of celebrating our 125th anniversary in lieu of the centenary that had been missed. By now, I had been president of Notre Dame for fifteen years and was deeply involved, as president for the past five years of the International Federation of Catholic Universities, in conducting meetings all over the world with the purpose of redefining the Catholic university. Vatican Council II was over. New thoughts were current everywhere in the church. I thought it would be a good time to restate what I thought Catholic universities should be doing, with Notre Dame as a natural focus because of its anniversary celebration. While I write specifically of Notre Dame, I was thinking more broadly of the ideal that we and others around the world were trying to achieve in our day. I like this formulation better than my earlier ones because it has a stronger focus and is more realistic or practical. I was becoming more immersed in worldwide problems by now and it begins to show.

There is a beginning of a declaration of independence here, too. This was the year that Notre Dame passed from clerical to lay control, an extremely important move. We were leaving an old world and creating a new one. This chapter also reflects the important statement on Catholic universities that a number of Catholic university presidents from Canada, the United States, and Latin America had formulated at Notre Dame's remote conference center in Land O'Lakes, Wisconsin, the previous July. I should also admit that after Vatican Council II, we were all feeling a bit feisty, but it was all to the good—and long overdue. Also, I think, it was a creative period for Catholic universities everywhere.

A decade later, it needs repeating. We are still a long way from realizing the vision, even though the vision is more commonly accepted today, and we are all seeking to make it a living reality.

III

The Vision of the Catholic University in the World of Today

One hundred and twenty-five years are not considered a very long time as the lives of great world universities are reckoned. I remember participating some years ago in the 600th anniversary of the University of Vienna. However, on the American scene, 125 years are considered to be a respectable age. Relatively few American universities are older than we at Notre Dame today.

One should not make too much, however, of this matter of age. Age alone is no real guarantee of quality unless one is considering red wine or cheese. Our present anniversary should be considered, I believe, rather as a grateful memorial to things past, an opportunity to assess things present, and, hopefully, a look to the future. The proud and cherished traditions of the past, in a fast-moving and ever-changing world, should always be a prelude to what this university might yet become.

A look at today and tomorrow for this university must take into full account the specific challenges and opportunities that we face as we ever try to create at Notre Dame a great Catholic university. Also, we cannot avoid facing frankly the dangers and difficulties that confront us along this road of present and future development. But neither should we be timid, unimaginative, or defensive. In fact, what we need most at this juncture of our history are all the qualities of the pioneer:

vision, courage, confidence, a great hope inspired by faith and ever revivified by love and dedication.

I hope that you are not shocked when I say that there has not been in recent centuries a truly great Catholic university, recognized universally as such. There are some universities that come very close to the reality, but not the full reality, at least as I see it in today's world. One might have hoped that history would have been different when one considers the church's early role in the founding of the first great universities in the Middle Ages: Paris, Oxford, Cambridge, Bologna, and others. They turned to the church for the charters that would guarantee them a freedom and autonomy they could not then have had from the state. Knowledge grew quickly within them because there was that new atmosphere of the free and often turbulent clashing of conflicting ideas, where a man with a new idea, theological, philosophical, legal, or scientific, had to defend it in the company of his peers, without interference from pressures and powers that neither create nor validate intellectual activity, one of God's greatest gifts to man.

This medieval conjunction of the church and the universities was to undergo a violent rupture in the years following the Reformation and, especially, the French Revolution. Philip Hughes, writing of this period, said: "Another grave loss was the disappearance of all the universities. They had been Catholic, and often Papal, foundations. In all of them there had been a faculty of theology, and round this mistress science their whole intellectual life had turned. Now they were gone, and when restored as State universities, [they became] academies for the exploration and exposition of natural truths alone. Education, the formation of the Catholic mind in the new Catholic Europe, would suffer immeasurably, and religious formation [would] be to its intellectual development an extra, something added on. There would be the further mischievous effect that henceforth not universities but seminaries would set the tone of theological life. The leaders of Catholic thought would not be the professional thinkers whom a university produces but technicians, those to whom the important work of training the future clergy is committed and who, among other things, teach them theology. The effect of this destruction of the faculties of theology in the universities of Catholic Europe, the disappearance of the old Salamanca, Alcala, Coimbra, Bologna, Donai, Louvain, and Paris, is a theme that still awaits its historian. Louvain was indeed restored in 1834, but the healthy interplay of the theological intellects of a half a score of Catholic universities, the Nineteenth Century was never, alas, to know."

What we are trying to do today in creating great Catholic universities is, in a sense, a recreation, so that the last third of the twentieth century will not suffer the loss which Philip Hughes bemoans for the nineteenth century and most of the twentieth. The comeback has begun in many places, Notre Dame being one of them. But this is happening in a much different world, and in a much different climate of opinion. Moreover, the university, as an institution, has developed in modern times into a much different reality than it was, even a little over a century ago when Cardinal Newman wrote his *Idea of a University*. That classic book can no longer be a complete model for the Catholic university of today. Also, one should reflect that Cardinal Newman never realized even in his day what he wrote about so well.

There are timeless principles in Newman's *Idea*, but he wrote about a completely different kind of university in a completely different kind of world. The *pax Britannica* and the colonies have given way to the newly independent and largely frustrated third world. The mainly rural world of the nineteenth century has now become largely urbanized. The population explosion has almost tripled world population in the last hundred years or so. Vatican I has been followed by Vatican II. We have progressively passed through two world wars and a whole series of brush wars, some unhappily still in progress. We have experienced an industrial, communications, nuclear, and space revolution. Ecumenism is supplanting many of the ancient and bitter religious and cultural rivalries. Never before has there been so much discussion and action about human rights and human development.

It is not surprising that universities have reflected increasingly in their structure and programs all of these revolutionary developments. Nowhere has this been more striking than in America. We inherited Newman's notion of the British university as an exclusive teaching institution, added on the concept of graduate and research functions from the German university model, and, to further complicate the institution, have elaborated since the end of World War II a new university function of service to mankind on the local, state, national, and international levels.

Apart from tripling the goals, the internal structure of the American university has undergone considerable change as well. Freedom and autonomy are still central to the university's life and spirit here and everywhere, but here they are buttressed by a system of governance that involves diverse layers of power and decision: boards of trustees, faculty, administration, alumni, and students. All are not equal members of this uneasy balance of power, but each group can and does have its say. Sir Eric Ashby has remarked in a recent book that the whole system is very complicated and very imperfect, but somehow it has worked and we have yet to find a better one.

This, then, in the briefest kind of shorthand, is the world into which the Catholic university is being reborn. One must remember that the church did not create this modern university world, as it helped create the medieval university world. Moreover, the church does not have to be present in this modern world of the university, but if it is to enter, the reality and the terms of this world are well established and must be observed. The terms may be complicated and unlike operating terms within the church itself. The reality of the university world may make the church uneasy at times, but all university people throughout the world recognize this reality and these terms as essential to anything that wishes to merit the name of university in the modern context. One may add descriptive adjectives to this or that university, calling it public or private, Catholic or Protestant, British or American, but the university must first and foremost be a university, or the qualifiers qualify something, but not a university.

I should add frankly at this time that many people in the university world and outside it take a dim view of the very possibility of a Catholic university. George Bernard Shaw put it most bluntly when he declared that a Catholic university is a contradiction in terms. I presume that he viewed the church of his day as an essentially closed society and the university as an essentially open society. This is a considerable over-simplification with which I shall deal later, given the developments of Vatican Council II. The core of the answer to Shaw must, of course, be that a university does not cease to be free because it is Catholic. Otherwise, I am not sure an answer is possible. It should also be said that the Catholic university is not the Catholic Church. It might be said to be *of* the church as it serves both the church and the people of God, but it certainly is not the magisterium. It is not the church teaching, but a place—the only place—in which Catholics and others, on the highest level of intellectual inquiry, seek out the relevance of the Christian message to all of the problems and opportunities that face modern man and his complex world.

I would be the last to claim that this Catholic university, or some other, will not at times be an embarrassment to the church or the hierarchy because of the actions of some faculty member, administrator, student, or a group of these. Universities have no monopoly on the misuse of freedom, but few institutions on earth need the climate of freedom to the extent that universities do, whatever the risk involved. Moreover, it should be said that universities since their founding in the Middle Ages have always been unruly places, almost by nature, since the university is the place where young people come of age—an often unruly process—places where the really important problems are freely discussed with all manner of solutions proposed, places where all the burning issues of the day are ventilated, even with hurricane winds at times. Again, by nature, the university has always been dedicated uniquely to criticism of itself and everything else, even, or perhaps especially, in the case of the Catholic university, those things held most dear.

The university is not the kind of place that one can or should try to rule by authority external to the university. The best and only traditional authority in the university is intellectual competence: this is the coin of the realm. This includes, in the

Catholic university especially, philosophical and theological competence. It was great wisdom in the medieval church to have university theologians judged solely by their theological peers in the university.

There will always be times when embarrassment might seem to be avoided by attempting to silence someone of unusual views or eccentric personality. Church and state share this temptation equally, with the church coming off better today, I believe. In most cases where this temptation is indulged, only greater embarrassment ultimately comes, especially to the cause of the university, the higher learning, the church, and the state. As Cardinal Newman said so well: "Great minds need elbow room, not indeed in the domain of faith, but of thought. And so indeed do lesser minds and all minds."

By now, it should be clear why we need the pioneering virtues mentioned above to attempt to create what to many seems impossible, a great Catholic university in our times. The time has come to define more positively just what we have in mind, no matter how difficult a task this is.

A great Catholic university must begin by being a great university that is also Catholic. What makes a great university in the ancient and modern tradition that we have been discussing? First and foremost, it must be a community of scholars, young and old, teaching and learning together, and together committed to the service of mankind in our times. It might be hoped that in a university worthy of the name the young learn from the old and vice versa, that the faculty grows wiser as it confronts the questioning, idealism, and generosity of each new generation of students, and that the students draw wisdom and perspective from their elders in the academic community. Any university should be a place where all the relevant questions are asked and where answers are elaborated in an atmosphere of freedom and responsible inquiry, where the young learn the great power of ideas and ideals, where the values of justice and charity, truth and beauty, are both taught and exemplified by the faculty, and where both faculty and students together are seized by a deep compassion for the anguishes of mankind in our day and committed to proffer a helping hand, wherever possible, in every aspect of man's material, intellectual, and cultural development. I believe that John Masefield, poet laureate of England, had all of this in mind when he wrote that the university is a splendid place. A great university must be splendidly all of this, or it is neither a university nor great. And let us candidly admit that many so-called universities today are neither.

Now the great Catholic university must be all of this and something more. If we at Notre Dame, today and tomorrow, can be all of this and something more, then the bottom drops out of the objections we have been considering. What is the something more? Here we can indeed take a page from Newman's book, where he says eloquently that there must be universality of knowledge within the university. Catholic means universal and the university, as Catholic, must be universal in a double sense: first, it must emphasize the centrality of philosophy and, especially, theology among its intellectual concerns, not just as window dressing, not just to fill a large gap in the total fabric of knowledge as represented in most modern university curricula. Rather, theology in the Catholic university must be engaged on the highest level of intellectual inquiry so that it may be in living dialogue with all the other disciplines in the university. Both philosophy and theology are concerned with the ultimate questions, both bear uniquely on the nature and destiny of man, and all human intellectual questions, if pursued far enough, reveal their philosophical and theological dimension of meaning and relevance. The university, as Catholic, must continue and deepen this dimension of intellectual discourse that was badly interrupted, to our loss, several centuries ago.

The second sense in which the Catholic university must be universal is related to the first, perhaps a corollary of its philosophical and theological concern. Without a deep concern for philosophy and theology, there is always the danger that the intellectual and moral aspects of all human knowledge become detached and separate. Technique can become central, rather than the human person, for whom technique is presumably a service. Social scientists can close their eyes to human values; physical scientists can be unconcerned with the use of the power they create. Stating all of this is not to say that all other knowledges in the Catholic university are ruled by a philosophical or theological imperialism. Each discipline has its own autonomy of method and its proper field of knowledge. The presence of philosophy and theology simply completes the total field of inquiry, raises additional and ultimate questions, moves every scholar to look beyond his immediate field of vision to the total landscape of God and man and the universe. One might turn the words of Shaw around and say that no university is truly a university unless it is catholic, or universal, in this sense.

Now may I bring all of this back to Notre Dame and our goals as we look ahead today? Some may worry a bit about what has just been said if it is phrased in terms of a commitment of this university as Catholic. I submit to you that we have overdone our fears about this word, commitment, which has become a kind of dirty word in university circles. Universities which exclude philosophy and theology as an integral part of the university education have also made a commitment. Some scholars are committed to agnosticism, atheism, scientism, humanism, and a whole host of other positions. Is our commitment less sacred or less permissible in the university world? Certainly not, if we make our commitment freely and intelligently. Should those who live peacefully with a host of alien commitments be denied their own? Should a commitment to wholeness and universality of knowledge by whatever means in an institution that calls itself a university be looked upon as retrogressive? I make no apology for any of my free commitments. I can live and work in the total academic community with all who profess other commitments. I only ask that it not be done in the name of uncommitment, which it is not, and that our intellectual respect for each other be mutual.

At Notre Dame, as in all universities, commitment to be meaningful must be personal rather than institutional, a thing of personal free conviction rather than institutional rhetoric. I think we have been able to do this at Notre Dame in a large, ecumenical fashion. Whatever the personal faith of our variegated faculty and student body, I have sensed that we are united in believing that intellectual virtues and moral values are important to life and to this institution. I take it that our total community commitment is to wisdom, which is something more than knowledge and much akin to goodness and beauty when it radiates throughout a human person.

If all of this is largely true, then I think that Notre Dame can perform a vital function in the whole wide spectrum of American higher learning, doing what many other institutions cannot or will not do. We can, in summary, give living witness to the wholeness of truth from all sources, both human and divine, while recognizing the inner sacredness of all truth from whatever source, and the validity and autonomy of all paths to truth. Somehow, the Notre Dame community should reflect profoundly, and with unashamed commitment, its belief in the existence of God and in God's total revelation to man, especially the Christian message; the deep, agelong mystery of salvation in history; the inner, inalienable dignity and rights of every individual human person, recognizing at the same time both man's God-given freedom and his human fallibility, an uneasy balance without God's grace; buttressing man's every move towards a more profound perception and articulation of truth and a more humane achievement of justice in our times—and Notre Dame must try to do all of this in the most ecumenical and open spirit. Somehow, all of this Judeo-Christian tradition should be reflected here at Notre Dame in the very humane atmosphere of this beautiful campus—in a spirit of civility as well as of love, in openness as well as in commitment, in our humble pilgrim search as well as in our enduring faith and hope. We may do all of this poorly, but we cannot, if we aspire to be a great Catholic university in the modern context, attempt to do less.

What kind of a place will Notre Dame be in the years ahead if all of this happens here? First, I think it will be a beacon, bringing to light, in modern focus, the wonderfully traditional and ancient adage: *intellectus quaerens fidem et fides quaerens intellectum*. How to say it for today? Let me begin by saying that modern man stands or cowers beneath a mushroom cloud. He has created it and in a sense it symbolizes all his efforts of self-destruction across all the ages. Yet he seeks a deeper meaning. Life cannot be simply negation and despair, so he seeks a faith: in God, in God's word, in God Incarnate in Christ Our Lord, in suffering and resurrection, in life eternal. These are the only realities that keep man today from the ultimate despair, suicide, either personal or global.

This is the faith that man seeks in this place, faith as a gift, faith that sets the mind of man to soaring beyond the limits of human intelligence, on the level of divine intelligence, into the realm of the beyond.

Intellectus quaerens fidem—the mind of man reaching out for a faith—this is one side of the coin. The other is *fides quaerens intellectum*: faith seeking in the university community an expression of belief that will be relevant to the uneasy mind of modern man. This means in a word that we cannot be satisfied here with medieval answers to modern questions. We cannot, for example, speak of war as if the bow and arrow had not been superseded by the nuclear intercontinental ballistic missile. Faith is unchangeable in what it believes, but as good Pope John said, there are many ways of expressing what we believe—and today, the words must be directed to the inner complexity of our times, as Manzoni said, in *I Promessi Sposi, guazzabuglio del cuore umano*: the utter confusion in the heart of man. The university is best prepared to understand this human confusion, and to speak to it with faithful words that say something, to avoid the meaningless formulae, the empty phrases, the words without weight. If the Catholic university can fulfill this first function of the human mind seeking faith, and faith reaching out for an expression adequate to our times, it will indeed be a great light in the all-encompassing darkness that engulfs our world today. Such a university will be faithful to the wisdom of the past, relevant to the present, and open to the future.

Secondly, the Catholic university must be a bridge across all the chasms that separate modern men from each other: the generational gap of the young and old, the rich and the poor, the black and the white, the believer and the unbeliever, the potent and the weak, the East and the West, the material and the spiritual, the scientist and the humanist, the developed and the less developed, and all the rest. To be such a mediator, the Catholic university, as universal, must have a foot and an interest in both worlds, to understand each, to encompass each in its total community and to build a bridge of understanding and love. Here the name of the game is peace, not conflict. Only in such a university community can the opposite sides discuss matters civilly, not shout at each other. Only in such a university community can there be the rational and civil discourse that builds bridges rather than widens the gulfs of misunderstanding. If this cannot be done here, then the human situation is hopeless, and we must resign ourselves to hatred, noise, violence, rancor, and, ultimately, the destruction of all we hold dear.

Thirdly, the Catholic university must be a crossroads where all the intellectual and moral currents of our times meet and are thoughtfully considered. How great is the need today for a place where dialogue is civil, not strident, where all ideas are welcome even if not espoused, where hospitality reigns for all who sincerely have something to say. Where else, except in the Catholic university, can the church confront the challenges, the anguishes, and the opportunities of our times? Where else can there be an *agora* such as that in which Saint Paul spoke of the unknown God in Athens?

Schema Thirteen of Vatican II addressed many problems of the church in the world today. This document is an invitation rather than an ultimate answer. If the ultimate answers are to be found, these must be found within the Catholic university community which is in living contact with the faith and the world, the problems and all the possible solutions, the possibilities and the despairs of modern man. In the modern Catholic university every sincere and thoughtful man should be welcome, listened to, and respected by a serious consideration of what he has to say about his belief or unbelief, his certainty or uncertainty. Here should be the home of the inquiring mind, and whatever the differences of religion, culture, race, or nationality, here should be the place where love and civility govern the conversation, the interest, and the outcome. Jacques Barzun called the university the house of the intellect. The Catholic university should, beyond all else, be this house, as well as the house of civility and lively discussion in the cause of truth, which unites us all in its quest and in its promise.

Let us now return to where we began: to the possibility of a great Catholic university in our times, since this is the ultimate challenge to Notre Dame on this occasion. I would like to describe one more dimension to the vision proposed above. Here, my guide is Father Teilhard de Chardin, a modern prophet despite the problems that attend his vision. Father Teilhard envisioned two parallel paths of human development: one natural that involved the humanization of all creation by man, another supernatural that would Christianize the total world. The natural goal was omega, the supernatural was called pleroma, or the recapitulation of all things in Christ, our Saviour. Teilhard believed that man would naturally give himself to the process of humanizing the world as we know it. This process would be attended by all manner of human frustration and despair, especially when all of the ambiguities and human negations bear upon man. For Teilhard, there was only one guarantee of human perseverance in the quest of natural progress: the parallel path of salvation history, of the grace of God in Christ, the deep belief that ultimately the omega and the pleroma would merge in the new creation. Otherwise, despite his deep belief in the evolutionary movement upward and onward, Teilhard knew nothing but despair.

I think we can find in this Teilhardian presentation an analogy or a prototype for the Catholic university. All universities are totally committed today to human development and human progress in the natural order of events. This whole endeavor is ultimately a fragile thing, left to itself, fraught frequently with frustration and often despair. Here in the total spectrum, the Catholic university does have something spectacular to offer. Call it faith, call it belief, call it a simple parallel course depending on other sources of strength, other sources of knowledge, a belief in an ultimate goal surpassing all natural endeavor. The Catholic university must be all that a university requires and something more. It may be that the Teilhardian parallel is the something more, the extra element that defies frustration and despair. However you measure it, we here commit ourselves to the something more, not in a triumphal spirit of being superior, but with the humble realization that we must be ourselves at Notre Dame, in keeping with our tradition, and that, hopefully, being ourselves will mean that we may add something to the total strength of what we most cherish: the great endeavor of the higher learning in our beloved America and in our total world. How more splendidly can we be a splendid place?

This chapter derives from an address to the Council of Protestant Colleges and Universities' meeting in Los Angeles ten years ago. The challenge faced then is no less real today. I hope I am not unduly harsh on Dr. Harvey Cox because I have generally enjoyed his writings and learned from them, with the exception of the chapter in question. As I get older, I think we all ought to be conceded a chancy chapter now and then, especially if we are speaking and writing often. The pressure is constant, and one tries to have an original good idea now and then, on a variety of subjects.

It is a good thought to remember occasionally that for the first centuries of American higher education, all of the institutions were religious in origin and commitment. This includes Harvard, as well as Yale, Princeton, and Dartmouth. The Methodists founded all of the following well-known universities: Boston, Duke, Emory, Northwestern, Southern Methodist, Syracuse, Denver, and Southern California.

One might question what happened to the religious commitment over the years. Each institution has its own tale to tell. One thing is certain: without that original commitment to Christian higher education, the total spectrum of American universities would be poorer today.

The following chapter tries to demonstrate that there is still a valid and important role to play for many of these institutions that still call themselves Christian.

IV

The Challenges of Christian Higher Education

Everyone is likely to agree that the 817 church-related colleges and universities in the United States face a future challenge. The only disagreement would be in the use of the word "future." Of course, equally great challenges face all the other private and public colleges and universities in this country. But our challenge is rather special, since it is encompassed in the broader challenge facing the churches themselves in modern America, with or without the colleges and universities they sponsor. We who live and work in Christian colleges and universities not only face a challenge, but we are also already under fire, as are our churches. One might best describe the challenge in its most dire terms as a challenge for survival. Those who predict our early demise do it about as discourteously as possible by saying that our institutions should never have been founded in the first place. Obviously then, for them, there is no point in continuing the farce. Even when it is granted that some of our institutions are among the top 10 percent in the nation academically, and are indeed admitted to be "America's unique contribution to higher education," Christian universities and colleges are said to struggle daily "with what to do about a 'church tradition' that usually seems less and less relevant to what they have to do to exist."

The critic I have been specifically quoting is Harvey Cox, writing in *The Secular City*, although I could have just as well quoted an unhappy Catholic, Dr. Rosemary Lauer [chairman

and professor of philosophy at San Diego State University],
who says that the church should get out of education. If you
prefer someone from neither camp, we can fall back on
George Bernard Shaw who said that a Catholic university is a
contradiction in terms.

Cox is perhaps the most widely read of all the current
critics, so let us first listen to his indictment in his own words,
again from *The Secular City* (New York: Macmillan, Inc., 1965):

> We have already noted that the university has always
> been a problem for the Church. But the current cleavage
> between the two is wider and more impassable than ever,
> precisely because we now stand at the end of the epoch of
> the Church's dominance in Western culture . . . (p. 219).
> The anachronistic posture of the Church is nowhere
> more obvious than in the context of the university commu-
> nity. The Church has made three attempts to come to terms
> with the university problem in America, all of which have
> been marked by a certain recidivism. The first was the
> establishment of its own colleges and universities. This, of
> course, is medievalism. The whole idea of a *Christian* col-
> lege or university after the breaking apart of the Medieval
> synthesis has little meaning. The term Christian is not one
> that can be used to refer to universities any more than to
> observatories or laboratories. No one of the so-called Chris-
> tian colleges that dot our Midwest is able to give a very
> plausible theological basis for retaining the equivocal
> phrase *Christian college* in the catalogue. Granted that there
> may be excellent traditional, public-relations, or sentimen-
> tal reasons for calling a college Christian, there are no
> theological reasons. The fact that it was founded by minis-
> ters, that it has a certain number of Christians on the faculty
> or in the student body, that chapel is required (or not
> required), or that it gets part of its bills paid by a
> denomination—none of these factors provides any
> grounds for labeling an institution with a word that the
> Bible applies only to followers of Christ, and then, very
> sparingly. The idea of developing "Christian universities"

in America was bankrupt even before it began (ibid., p. 221).

I spare you the full flavor of his rhetoric on the other two means by which the churches came to terms with the university problem in America. The second means was "residential congregations to render a special ministry to people involved in university life"; the third was "to transplant onto the university campus a denominational church disguised as a 'house' with ping-pong tables and a less ministerial minister." He adds later that "we are still in the third phase of this cumulative catastrophe." Apparently, we dinosaurs of the first unhappy phase are already written off and forgotten. Should we now curl up and die?

Later on in this chapter on the church and the university, Cox describes three functions that the church should be undertaking that require "stepping out of the organizational shells in which they are imprisoned on the hinterlands of the campus [and even more so I would gather, stepping out of so-called Christian colleges and universities, the worst anachronism of all] and [stepping] into the university community itself." The three functions Cox elaborates are: (1) restrained reconciliation; (2) candid criticism; and (3) creative disaffiliation. I would like to suggest that there is great and even greater validity in pursuing these three churchly functions within the Christian college and university; indeed, that these three functions need doing there first and foremost, if the total college and university community in America is to be spared much of what Cox forecasts. I would gladly admit that our Christian colleges and universities need desperately to find themselves, their identity, their special function and high purpose in the totality of American higher education. Maybe Cox has inadvertently helped us in this most important endeavor.

Obviously, I do not intend to apply these three functions in the same context that he does, in the secular university community, since my point is quite apart from his, namely, having accepted the importance of these three functions, they do have a true home and even greater validity within the context of the Christian college and university, especially as these institutions validate their own proper existence and influence the total collegiate and university community in modern-day America. In other words, I grant his substance, but apply his functions quite differently, still I trust with no less, but even greater, ultimate and total effect.

1. *Reconciliation.* Cox's biblical text for this function is good, although there are many other texts which would illuminate and complement it: "God was in Christ reconciling the world to Himself. And we are ministers of reconciliation." Cox adds: "The Church has no purpose other than to make known to the world what God has done and is doing in history to break down the hostilities between men and to reconcile men to each other." Again good, but not far enough. We reconcile men to each other *in Christ and in his love.* The history of salvation is what the church is about, and this has reference not only between men, but, even more importantly, also between men and God. Reconciliation is not the only term for this priestly responsibility. It is even more essentially a work of mediation, for the priest is essentially a mediator, a *pontifex,* a bridge-builder. The mediation of God's message to every age must somehow go on, and it is precisely to do this work of mediation that Christian colleges and universities were founded and exist today. They not only transmit to every age the totality of human knowledge in the humanities, in the social and physical sciences, in the professions, but they do it in the context of the Christian saving message. They also do it in the context of the Christian community, in which Christian love is the moving force of reconciliation, and they bolster their efforts by research and vital teaching so that mediation may be continually more effective as knowledge widens. They mediate also by community prayer, wherein we admit how little we have really understood the Christian message, yet how very much we do wish to obtain the grace of greater understanding and ultimate wisdom, and, finally, they mediate in Christian service, where all our misunderstandings are caught up and redeemed by the Christian giving of ourselves and all we have to others in Christ.

Let it be admitted that we do all of this all too poorly, too unimaginatively, and too ungenerously, but at least our attempts are honest, and perhaps that alone justifies the calling of our colleges and universities Christian. If I might be medieval for a moment, the notion of analogy was then and is now a valid description of the use of words. I do not take the notion of Christian college or university as equivocal, in Cox's terms, but analogical, in the simple sense that what the Bible implies of a person by calling him Christian, that too applies to our institutions, albeit imperfectly, as followers of Christ. It is the spirit that is important here, the intent, the dedication, the commitment. Our institutions, if we try to mediate the saving work of Christ in all we do, are no less Christian than Christian art, or Christian music, or Christian culture. To speak of Christian observatories or laboratories is Cox's point, not ours. We grant his point, but add that it only obfuscates this very real issue of Christian colleges and universities.

The mediator stands in the middle, but he stands for something, else he is a mighty poor mediator. Our Christian institutions are mediators between the believing and the unbelieving, the devout and the tepid, the dedicated and the uncommitted, the knowing (in the Christian sense) and the ignorant, between those who think the Christian context is important and those who think it negligible. At least we stand for a point of view—in history, in philosophy, in theology, in literature, in art, in music, in drama, in the use of science and technology, in the nature and destiny of man. We know that God has spoken to man and we think this important enough to be reckoned with in all else we know, or believe we know, from whatever source. And we are not about to abdicate the field, whatever Cox says about "the end of the epoch of the Church's dominance in Western culture."

We know that our culture would be poorer today without all that the church, or better, Christ and His message of salvation and faith and hope and charity have brought to it. We are not interested in dominance. We are ready to mediate Christ's message to all forms of human knowledge in institutions sympathetic to the message, our Christian colleges and universities and outside them, too, within the broader collegiate and university context. Ours is not the concept of a ghetto, but a leaven and a light in the darkness. These images are also biblical. And we apologize to no audience for the weakness of our efforts in view of the greatness of that which we presume to mediate. We are unfaithful servants if we do not try ever to mediate better, despite the difficulty of the age. Whoever is against us, we might at least assume that Christ and the history of salvation are with us. Thus we proudly, and humbly, bear the name of Christian, ourselves and our institutions.

2. *Creative Criticism.* Under this rubric, Cox calls for criticism of both the university and the church. In regard to the university, he is against any world view as being divisive. Here I am reminded of the divisiveness of Christ: you are either with Me or against Me. Again I am reminded of the testimony of two professors, former Danforth Fellows, at a Catholic and a Presbyterian college, contained in the Patillo-Mackenzie report on church-sponsored higher education:

Although it may sound paradoxical, I, as a faculty member, feel freer in the Church-related institutions (all Roman Catholic) with which I am familiar. It is a freedom to be myself—to explore and to communicate whatever religious dimensions I, as a religiously oriented person, find or fail to find within my discipline. I did not feel this same freedom when I taught at non-Church-related institutions, committed, as the faculty and student bodies seemed to be, to a secular materialistic humanism. I found myself squashing areas of investigation and perceptions of religious significance in literature which would have been either totally misunderstood or ridiculed in the secular environment. In the Church-related college, religious meanings and interpretations are understood and encouraged without—and obviously this is essential—forcing them where they do not fit. So, to oversimplify it, *both* the religious and the secular are admitted to the Church-related institution, while *only* the secular is admitted in the secular institution. The result I find to be a greater sense of exploration, a freer intellectual atmosphere, and a greater opportunity to find truth. And from the vantage point of within a Church-related college, I feel freer to criticize the failings of my Church.

The second professor was in the process of moving from a Presbyterian college to a larger state university. He writes:

> Let me close by noting an additional satisfaction of teaching in the Christian college which I think may be inherent in that type of institution and hard to find in other types of colleges. It is easy to find other scholars who are interested in the question of how their disciplines and professions relate to the Christian way of life and the Christian faith. One can talk directly and overtly about those questions, rather than obliquely as I anticipate doing at a state university.

In citing these two professors, I am not attempting to demonstrate that all is rosy and Christlike at our institutions. Even less am I trying to resuscitate the old antagonism between Christian and state institutions in which the latter are characterized as "Godless." When over 40 percent of state universities today are sponsoring some type of course in religion, it seems to me that with the advantage of the general acceptance of the Christian philosophy of life, in the broadest, most liberal, most ecumenical and open sense of that phrase, in most of our Christian institutions, our most creative criticism of the contemporary scene in higher education would be to demonstrate the meaningfulness of whatever integration and unity of knowledge we have been able to achieve in mediation, in the hope that it will be contagious, not divisive.

As regards criticism of our churches, again I do not know where this can be done in a more understanding and creative sense than on our campuses. Here, as nowhere else, the church meets the contemporary world. I fully agree with the recommendations of Patillo and Mackenzie when they say:

> In our judgment, the faculties of Church-related colleges are in the most favorable position to provide intellectual

leadership in the study of the issues facing the Church and the hammering out of proposals for action. The Church college lives in both the "Church world" and the "outside world." Its faculty, in the aggregate, has the breadth of knowledge required to see the Church in perspective. College faculties include historians, philosophers, artists, theologians, psychologists, sociologists, literary critics, political scientists, economists—scholars whose business it is to be sensitive to ideas and to understand the meaning of the world around us. They are in touch with secular thought, but at their best they care about the Church and its future.

Needless to say, the church will not receive this kind of creative criticism from the faculty and students of its colleges and universities unless it allows them a maximum freedom to be creative and critical. The church has nothing to fear from criticism springing from those who love the church, who want to participate as fully as possible in the continual reformation by which the church faces each new age and each new problem, by which the church continually renews herself and purges herself of her many earthly imperfections which are a denial of her total dedication to Christ Our Lord and His saving message. I strongly believe that in default of strong, intelligent, dedicated, and creative criticism within the church, and especially from within the church's institutions of higher learning, the church will suffer the worst kind of carping, sniping, vindictive, and, to say the worst, unloving criticism from those who have already written off the church, whose unspoken motto seems to be, *écrasez l'infâme*—wipe out the infamy. In a word, if the prophetic, creatively critical mission of the church-related institution of higher learning is not vital and courageous, the priestly, mediatorial mission will be diminished, even more, in a true and valid sense, suspect. There then would be no easier option for the generality of mankind but to write off the Christian college and university as Cox has done.

3. *Creative Disaffiliation*. This third function suggested by Cox is the most difficult to apply to our context, instead of his,

but it is possible and fruitful, too. First, Cox describes creative disaffiliation as "the modern equivalent of asceticism, the focusing of energy on what is important at the cost of denying what is less important." No problem here.

Consistent with his earlier stance, Cox sees the churches as hindered in their work by "ingrown isolation made unavoidable by the sheer size and complexity of the apparatus and by an institutional and social conservatism related to their dependence on sources of funds, a dependence which in turn precludes the possibility of any real criticism of the structural elements in our society."

His advice then is to disaffiliate from this bureaucratic monstrosity. "The university Christian who succumbs to the temptation of work within the organizational Church stands in deadly danger of cutting himself off from the reconciliatory action of God in the world and blinding himself to his place in the drama through which action is taking place." As to the church itself, he asks in the concluding paragraph of this chapter, "What is the role of the Church in the university? The 'organizational Church' has no role. It should stay out."

As I wrote earlier, it is difficult to apply Cox's third function of "creative disaffiliation" to our context, since he has earlier eliminated our context. He is speaking here of the church and the Christian in the secular university. What I say here depends largely on what I have already said, following his lead in a secular context, on the priestly and prophetic functions of the Christian college and university. One more point must be made here. However one speaks of the church, as a visible or invisible body, or as both, the Christian college and university are not the church. And they are very much in the world. We should indeed disaffiliate ourselves from any influence that is not ecumenical, that cuts us off from each other or from the world, or from the very real values that are to be derived from a wider understanding of all the social revolutions in progress.

No age has seen a greater dedication to human dignity, human equality, and human development than our own. No age has had greater resources, educational, scientific, technical, and human, to do something about these deepest of human aspirations. Our Christian colleges and universities might well disaffiliate ourselves from our more bland and imitative educational endeavors to throw the full weight of our Christian intelligence and educational dedication into these secular revolutions, which may indeed be close to the heart of the mystery of salvation in our times. We have no need to disaffiliate from the church or from our Christian institutions to do this, but we must respect the validity of new knowledge and new techniques and, relatively, new aspirations. We must understand them on their own terms.

All truth is a part of God's redemptive activity, but all grace is too. And grace, for us at least, comes from another source. Ultimately, both all truth and all grace are from God. More immediately, we seek, find, and respect secular truth in all our institutions of higher learning. We, in Christian institutions, also seek an ever greater understanding of the meaning and relevance of God's divine word from his revelation. We seek this grace particularly in our Christian institutions of higher learning to inspire, to refresh, and to revivify all our efforts to find and understand all his saving truth in the modern context.

No single facet of this total reality of truth and grace need be denied, nor should any or all of it be confused or underestimated or eliminated, even in an essay as novel and insightful as *The Secular City*. There are indeed changing social structures and new functional arrangements following upon the spread of secularization in the world at large and in the world of the intellect. But the lineaments of Jesus Christ and his saving message of grace and truth are yesterday, today, and tomorrow, ever the same.

There may well be new and effective methods of witness in our age. We need not deny them, but in affirming them there is even less need to destroy what in its own unique way may ultimately be more effective, as I believe Christian higher education to be. As the old saw goes, "Don't throw out the baby with the bath."

If Harvey Cox has spurred us to take a deeper look at ourselves, as Christians, and at our institutions of higher learning, as professedly Christian, if he has piqued us enough to make us redouble our efforts to do more pointedly, more energetically, and with greater focus, the important work we are concerned with in all of our waking hours, then I think we should be grateful to him, even if this was not one of the purposes he had in mind.

At the heart of our specific endeavor are two great educational qualities: commitment and freedom. Have no fear of commitment as long as it is intelligent and deeply believes on real evidence the truth of those great Christian values to which we are committed. Have no fear of freedom either. It is the context within which commitment grows, deepens and is enriched, as we freely seek a greater dimension of understanding, a broader unity within the total reality we know, and a better expression of all these values that will speak to the heart of modern humanity in words that they, too, will understand and appreciate. There are all kinds of commitment in the world of higher learning today, scientific, secular, humanistic, agnostic, and all the rest. No one makes any apology for them. We must not be less free than any of them, or less committed. We must even grant them more freedom than they grant us, believing that ultimately the truth makes all of us most free.

Sometimes a fact is much more important than many words. When, through some great good fortune, the American Association of University Professors named me winner of their 1970 Alexander Meiklejohn Award for Academic Freedom, it seemed appropriate to enunciate to the university world at large the principles of academic freedom that I had been voicing so loudly within the Catholic university world.

We were not the only one with problems. Freedom will always be a problem for everyone, especially so in the university world. Whenever we get troublesome, which is almost always when we are doing our critical best, someone gets the bright idea of imposing controls. As an example, the first thing that the new military government in Chile did after deposing Allende was to put admirals in charge of each university. When I met the one who was trying to run the Catholic University in Santiago, I asked him, "Since you would be upset if I tried to tell you how to run the navy, what makes you think you know anything about running a university?" He said, "It was out of control. I am just purifying it."

Purify us and we die. Long live academic freedom. I have added a few cautions here, but not regarding purification.

V

The Catholic University and Freedom

The Alexander Meiklejohn Award for Academic Freedom calls our attention to at least two things: first, that academic freedom is by no means a new concern in higher education. Safeguarding academic freedom has been a constant struggle in higher education since universities began and, in the broader sense, since men began to teach one another. In this connection, may I congratulate the American Association of University Professors on its eternal vigilance. I should like to say another word later on the special need for that vigilance today. Second, the award, by its very name, reminds us that American higher education has been blessed in its history with a number of educational giants, men of exceptional vision, energy, and talent, to whom we are all greatly indebted. Alexander Meiklejohn, who as president of Amherst College marked out some of the fundamental directions for liberal education, is among them.

I note from the list of previous winners of this award that I am the first representative of a Catholic university to be so honored. As a priest and theologian, I thought I might comment about the special meaning that academic freedom has for us in a Catholic university. Perhaps because of certain historical misunderstandings, we in the Catholic universities particularly are more sensitive to possible infringements on academic freedom than those who have not shared the same experiences and fought the same battles.

Academic freedom, like all freedom, is grounded ultimately in the nature of man and of society and of the development of knowledge and intelligence. Man's greatest genius and dignity, as well as his last best hope, are in his intellect and in his search for truth. In an imperfect and fallible world, man cannot, in fact, be man—he cannot be true to himself—unless he is free to follow any argument, any research, any point of inquiry, wherever it may lead. Those in the academy must be free to share their convictions and responsible conclusions with their colleagues and students, in their teaching and in their writing, without fear of reprisal.

Even if it should want to, which, of course, it does not, the church could not impose its theological system on anyone. To accept the teaching of the church is a free act or it is nothing at all. There is no conflict between the goals of the church and those of the university. These goals and objectives, in fact, complement one another. As was pointed out by Vatican Council II: "The Church recalls to the mind of all that culture must be made to bear on the integral perfection of the human person, and on the good of the community and the whole of society. Therefore, the human spirit must be cultivated in such a way that there results a growth in its ability to wonder, to understand, to contemplate, to make personal judgments, and to develop a religious, moral, and social sense."

At the close of Vatican Council II, it seemed important to me—in another capacity as president of the International Federation of Catholic Universities—to have Catholic universities worldwide clarify their commitment to academic freedom. We began by a meeting of North American representatives at Notre Dame's retreat in northern Wisconsin. This resulted in what has come to be known as the 1967 Land O'Lakes Statement. I quote three short passages from that statement:

> The Catholic university today must be a university in the full modern sense of the word, with a strong commitment to and concern for academic excellence. To perform its teaching and research functions effectively, the Catholic university must have a true autonomy and academic free-

dom in the face of authority of whatever kind, lay or clerical, external to the academic community itself. To say this is simply to assert that institutional autonomy and academic freedom are essential conditions of life and growth and indeed of survival for Catholic universities as for all universities.

In a Catholic university all recognized university areas of study are frankly and fully accepted and their internal autonomy affirmed and guaranteed. There must be no theological or philosophical imperialism; all scientific and disciplinary methods, and methodologies, must be given due honor and respect. However, there will necessarily result from the interdisciplinary discussions an awareness that there is a philosophical and theological dimension to most intellectual subjects when they are pursued far enough. Hence, in a Catholic university there will be a special interest in interdisciplinary problems and relationships.

The student must come to a basic understanding of the actual world in which he lives today. This means that the intellectual campus of a Catholic university has no boundaries and no barriers. It draws knowledge and understanding from all the traditions of mankind; it explores the insights and achievements of the great men of every age; it looks to the current frontiers of advancing knowledge and brings all the results to bear relevantly on man's life today. The whole world of knowledge and ideas must be open to the student; there must be no outlawed books or subjects. Thus the student will be able to develop his own capabilities and to fulfill himself by using the intellectual resources presented to him.

But academic freedom does not live by rhetoric alone. Each year brings its new crisis. When the battle seems newly won, hostilities break out on another front. It is not so much that freedom is fragile as that it must be won daily, and exercised daily and responsibly, by each one of us. Let me pose two questions which confront us: (1) Are we making the best use of our academic freedom today? (2) Is the world around us developing a climate in which our freedom within will be increasingly disrespected, threatened, diminished, and, if possible, extinguished from without? I believe that the two questions are not unrelated. In fact, if we answer the first question badly, we almost guarantee a bad answer to the second question.

As to the first, we need often to be reminded that academic freedom is not so much freedom *from somebody or something*, as freedom to do something, which raises the whole question of what universities should be doing today with their freedom. Alexander Meiklejohn might come back to haunt me if I did not insist here that we use our freedom to do something creative and imaginative to reform and revivify liberal education, which should be at once the guarantee and the crowning achievement of academic freedom. But beyond this urgent and general task that faces us, what of the particular use of our freedom to view our society critically and to exercise our best moral judgment on a whole host of pressing modern topics: the sacredness of human life, the dignity of man, human rights and human equality, the uses of science and technology, war and peace, violence and nonviolence, human as well as physical pollution, the quality, meaning, condition, and effectiveness of academic life, academic commitment, academic protest or protestation or, at times, posturing as we confront these vital issues which sometimes seem more important to our students than they do to us? I am not suggesting the politicization of the university, but as a professional class of university men and women, do we effectively bring to our times the wisdom, the insight, the courage, and the moral judgment that should characterize our profession?

As to the second question, I am reminded that recently a majority of Americans in a CBS News nationwide poll appeared willing to cancel five of the ten guarantees of our Bill of Rights. As James Reston observed in the *New York Times*, "The uses of physical violence against the people, property, and institutions of the United States in defiance of the law have created a climate of fear in the country, and under the dominion of fear, a great many people now seem willing to choose order at the expense of their liberties, or at least at the expense of somebody else's liberties."

The times call for vision and leadership to an extraordinary degree, and hope as well. The French have a saying that "fear is a poor counselor." I suppose that the obverse of that is a call to each of us to use our freedom with courage and, hopefully, with wisdom.

The National Catholic Educational Association in 1969 asked me back for another keynoter. Much had changed in the brief eight years since I had last addressed them. I like to believe that all of us matured in adversity, of which we had plenty during those years. This chapter brings together so many of the things that had been stirring within me and happening, too.

Change had fascinated me since the early days of studying philosophy. One of the first university talks I gave was at the University of Chicago on the subject "Change and the Changeless." I did not realize at that time how much change was in store for us and our world, but somehow, pondering the necessity of stability in the face of change, seeing change as growth and forward movement, was good preparation for what was to come.

Change has a destabilizing effect on many people and many institutions. It seemed important at this moment to insist with my colleagues in Catholic higher education that we should take a good positive look at the changes all around us and ahead of us in order to grow and progress, rather than despair and fall apart.

After looking at change in general, I take a new look at what it means for the governance of our universities, for our faculties and students. There are many familiar themes here and many to which I will return in the pages yet to come. By now, the reader will have a good idea of what concerns me most: vision, values, change, freedom, relevance, and academic openness to a new day, ever aborning.

VI

The Changing Face of Catholic Higher Education

Change has often been described as a condition of life—what does not change, dies. If this is so, then Catholic higher education is very much alive today; in fact, for us change has not in recent years been just a condition, but rather a way of life. If many of our institutions' founding fathers were to return for a visit today, they would not recognize their creations. Some would be pleasantly surprised, some shocked, some probably horrified.

There are three main foci for the basic changes in Catholic higher education today: trustees, faculty, and students. There are, of course, many subsidiary wheels within wheels, but I shall attempt to mention them in passing. However, I am convinced that the really significant changes are structural, with the understanding that the basic ideas behind the structural changes will be operative in the new structures. I am not assuming that this is necessarily so, but I do assume that new ideas are generally more operative within new structures than without them. In a very real sense, new structures institutionalize new ideas. Here is the very core of change and a new life-style.

For all its revolutionary implications, the change from clerical to lay trustees was effected in a few institutions with a minimum of fuss and all too little publicity. It is a move that still lies ahead for most Catholic institutions of higher learning and other Catholic institutions, such as hospitals, although I cannot overemphasize its basic importance to any significant change.

I believe, immodestly, that Saint Louis and Notre Dame established the basic pattern at about the same time. We are two of the largest institutions in the whole Catholic Church. We were completely under clerical control for all our history, and then in May and June of 1967, we passed into lay control. This was not a legal fiction or a trick with mirrors. If anyone owns these multimillion-dollar institutions, the largest of their kind, it is now laymen, not priests or religious orders.

At Notre Dame, the laymen make the basic policy decisions under new statutes which clearly and for the first time declare our Catholicity under a state charter; they appoint the president and principal officers; they approve and publish the budget; they answer to any and all public and church authority, although they are largely independent of both.

All of this was not accomplished without protest or large cries of anguish on the part of a few who profess poverty, but cling to possessions; who profess the Christian education of the whole man, but would deny to their own graduates the responsibility for a Catholic institution; who profess service, but want to govern; who profess humility, but want power. Perhaps I am too blunt, but just attempt to do what we did, and you will find the same reaction from those to whom any basic change is anathema.

All that Father Paul Reinert of Saint Louis and I can tell you is that our lay trustees have given great strength and dedication to our institutions. They are no less Catholic than we; sometimes possibly more so. We have more freedom for good and honest intellectual endeavor than ever before. We have more moral and financial support. Our special juridical and institutional status is much more visible and clean-cut vis-à-vis the church and the state. We have more freedom for untrammeled' priestly and religious service, less ambiguity about the good of the institution and the good of the order. There is more visibility to the considerable services that we, as religious, are contributing and more dignity to those who serve because their competency is recognized. Professionalism is the new emphasis, not blind and often uncomprehending or mechanical or unmotivated obedience. In a word, we are vastly better off in every way.

I can honestly think of nothing bad and everything good to say about this new arrangement for the highest governance of the Catholic college or university. Perhaps a little less than two years is too short a time in which to pass judgment, but, thus far, all systems are go and the total effect has been very good indeed. I am personally grateful to the vision of our highest religious authorities and our religious confreres for making all of this possible, and to our lay trustees for accepting this serious responsibility at great personal cost to themselves, their time and talents. What I find slightly incredible is that so many institutions with even greater problems have been so slow to do likewise. This is, of course, their business, not mine, but I must say in frankness that the time to act is not now, but long past.

There are some structural changes that are difficult to judge. This one, I think, speaks for itself. This new form of governance has solved, once and for all time, the problem of academic freedom within the Catholic university. And it has removed from the bishops and the magisterium of the church all the possible embarrassments that can come from an institution that is totally in the service of the church without being the church or the magisterium. The Catholic university, thus conceived, operates as a civil corporation, under a state charter and lay control, thus becoming an extraordinarily effective bridge between the church and the world. It truly answers to both and is organizationally directly responsible to neither. If it does its task properly, it should be a blessing to both.

I am assuming here the kind of vision described above, but I can attest that this kind of vision is available to those who will match it to the structural changes I have been describing. There is a curious kind of clericalism that assumes that only clerics have vision. If this were true, it would signify the failure of our whole higher educational effort—but, fortunately, it is not true. In fact, I believe we need a double vision today, that of clerics and laymen working together, and I know of no place where this can be better done than in the field of Catholic higher education.

This is as good a spot as any to pass on to the second focus for change, the faculty of Catholic higher education. There was, in the recent past, no organization in the world where the president had more power and more control than in the Catholic college or university. He moderated all worlds there: the material, the intellectual, the spiritual. This situation is long gone in the better Catholic institutions of higher learning and, in large measure, explains why they are now better. One-man rule in the church and its organizations had its last gasp theoretically when collegiality was proclaimed, in Vatican Council II. One might hope that earlier developments in Catholic higher education both promoted and were confirmed by this proclamation of collegiality.

For too long a time, lay professors and even lay administrators in Catholic colleges and universities felt themselves to be second-class citizens, the hired hands who did the work, but made none of the decisions. The first official decision of our new lay board of trustees was to confirm the yearlong study of our faculty—like most, more than 90 percent lay— and to approve the provisions of a new faculty manual which clearly places all academic decisions in the hands of all the faculty and their elected representatives on the various councils and senate.

For once and for all, all the i's were dotted and all the t's crossed. Nothing is left to chance or to the beneficence of a philosopher-king-president. Appointments, promotion, tenure, curriculum, academic freedom and autonomy, due process, professional standards, and all the rest—these, the trustees decided, were the realm of the faculty and to be determined on the terms and according to the procedures that the faculty specified in its yearlong study.

Professionalism and competence are the coin of this realm. Again, there is no first-class institution of higher learning where this is not the order of the day. Moreover, in Catholic institutions, there was an interesting twist of reverse English—when all of these rights and duties and responsibilities were legislated by the faculty, for the faculty, it was clearly stated that all clerical faculty should enjoy them to the same extent as lay faculty, that as professional men, all should be accorded equal dignity and freedom.

All this will sound strange to other secular institutions who so legislated their affairs several decades ago, but again, this must be seen against the background of change in the church and its institutions already discussed above. The important point now is not that these changes were a long time in coming, but that they are here, completely and wholeheartedly here, and that our institutions are immeasurably better and stronger because of this basic structural change. Coming of age is a happy event, whenever and however and wherever it happens.

There are two other matters I should mention in regard to faculty. First, I think Catholic institutions of higher learning have always had, long before faculty manuals, a very special kind of faculty. Maybe it was a case of self-selection, maybe we fared better than we deserved, but the lay faculty I have known in Catholic colleges and universities over the years always seemed to have a special kind of dedication, a zest for teaching all too uncommon today, and a loyalty to the institution. They were most often the kind of persons we felt happy at seeing as the preceptors of the next generation, because they were unselfish, dedicated, and good, as well as wise, people.

The day of Mr. Chips is probably long gone, a casualty to publish-or-perish, but may I say that in the changeover to greater professionalism, I hope that we still will have the good sense to cherish this vanishing type of professor who enjoys professing, in his teaching and in his life, every good thing that we would like to think characterizes the life of the mind that is not divorced from the life of the heart, the good person who teaches more by what he is than by what he says.

I do not think that change towards professionalism need involve a disregard for what a person is, as well as what he knows, what degrees he holds. There are still great and intelligent and well-educated persons who are attracted to institutions that stand for something, as we should. Only they can make our institutions what they profess to be. May we continue to seek them out, cherish them, and listen to them, for they are the unsung heroes of days gone by. They may still be heroes today, perhaps less unsung, but we need them. May I also say in honest tribute that many of them were not and are not Catholic, even though they have cherished everything that the word Catholic, at its best, stands for. They are at home with us, and we have had a better home of the intellect because of their presence. They made ecumenism a reality in Catholic institutions of higher learning long before most people knew what the word meant.

The second matter that needs inclusion in the record is something that, no matter what we say, is always a matter of open suspicion to all who really do not know what Catholic higher education is and can be. This is the matter of freedom and autonomy. No matter what many professors, Catholic and non-Catholic, who have taught with us and in other types of universities, say regarding the complete freedom and autonomy they find in our institutions, there is always the lurking suspicion that somehow a Catholic college or university cannot really be free and autonomous. We seem to be tagged with thought control no matter what we say or do. Our faculty manuals may assure as much and more than others, our faculty may testify to the fact, but always there is the assumption that being Catholic means being unfree.

It matters not that one may feel uneasy in mentioning spiritual matters in other secular institutions. Commitment to the importance of the spiritual and moral implications of all human questions, to make the discussion truly complete and adequate, is seen as a fault, whereas commitment to anything else—atheism, agnosticism, secular humanism, materialism, or whatever—is seen as a virtue of sorts. I suppose all we can really do is to keep on saying that no subject, no intellectual approach to a question, no book, or no speaker is out of bounds on our campuses, whenever it is a question of honest and intelligent discussion. We can still insist on the fundamental importance of philosophical and theological dimensions, for as Riesman and Jencks say, this may be our special contribution to the American intellectual scene: to insist on the consideration and discussion of ultimate questions and ultimate values.

The real crux of this question of academic freedom and

autonomy in Catholic institutions of higher learning is not ultimately in political science or literature or chemistry, but in theology. Here our past record, especially in America, is not too spectacular, not because of overt oppression, but because our institutions have not distinguished themselves in theology. But this, too, is changing, and a crisis of credibility may be in the offing.

Here is the real testing ground, the real confrontation between the church teaching—the magisterium—which we are not, and the pilgrim church seeking a deeper understanding and expression of revealed truth, which we very much are.

The gist of my thesis is this: theology in the Catholic university must enjoy the same freedom and autonomy as any other university subject because, otherwise, it will not be accepted as a university discipline and without its vital presence, in free dialogue with all other university disciplines, the university will never really be Catholic.

I grant the difference between teaching Catholic doctrine to undergraduates—which should not be unlike teaching classical physics or mathematics or history—and doing graduate research. In the latter endeavor, there may at times be a real or apparent conflict between the magisterium of the bishops and the hypotheses of the pioneer university theologian working at the frontiers of theological inquiry. I see no problem in bishops saying on occasion that, in their judgment, the theologian is not being faithful to the accepted teaching or expression of revealed truth, but they can do this without seeming to jeopardize his honest efforts within the authentic realm of university research, which is something different from teaching revealed truths.

Now to students, always the most exciting and the most difficult part of any educational discussion today. Here, change is not only rampant, but also galloping. First let us say, God bless them, these difficult, demanding, revolutionary students who are the reason and often the despair of our educational existence. We find it difficult to live with them, but, without them, there would be little reason for our institutions. They are the wave of the future that threatens to engulf the present, namely us. But we have to understand them, even more, to love them—else we should abandon the whole endeavor. So let us try.

If the name of the game is change, today, for students of this generation, the name is *changissimus*. Whatever is must go, and whatever is not must come to be. I am less than convinced by this general persuasion, but in view of what I have already said, I can understand it. A few examples may elucidate the problem.

First, there is the drive for relevancy in all that is taught in our institutions today. Here, I smell an easy error, and a deep and abiding truth. If relevancy means that education must prepare one to live and operate in a real world, as opposed to an imaginary world, who can oppose it? But if relevancy is confused with contemporaneity, then we are being hoaxed, and so are the students. What is relevant today—such as today's newspaper—is completely irrelevant next week, next month, and, especially, next year. Relevancy certainly has to have reference to the present, anchors in the past, and meaning for the future. To this extent, it is geared to that which is unchanging—truth and falsehood, good and evil, life and death, beauty and ugliness, justice and injustice, time and eternity, love and hate, war and peace—to mention a few of the really relevant issues that have faced mankind yesterday, today, and certainly will face him tomorrow. All of these issues will be relevant if we have a colony of human beings on Mars by the year 2000.

If the university is not to amuse or distract, rather than to educate its students, it must resist a superficial *nowness* of concern, a relevancy of today that passes all too quickly with tomorrow, a relevancy that will all too soon be a monumental irrelevancy. Certainly, man can learn something from the human victories and failures of the past, can measure against them the problems of the present, and can rationally and hopefully face the future armed with this knowledge. I spare you Santayana's dictum about those who ignore history. Even in such a pragmatic and relevant subject as civil engineering, the half-life of all that can be learned today, with the most up-to-date knowledge and techniques, is ten years. In other words, the best and most relevant of civil engineering science today is 50 percent irrelevant ten years from now. This is inevitable with all of human knowledge doubling every fifteen years.

Here again, the Catholic college and university can lead the way amid shifting sands, if we have the courage to insist that there are philosophical and theological realities, bearing on the nature and destiny of man, that have a much longer half-life, in fact a life stretching into eternity. What is more relevant than man himself, with his visions and his failures, with his grace and his ugliness, with his promise and his disappointments? History and literature, philosophy and theology, poetry, art, and drama, language, law, and culture—these are the subjects that retain across all the years their relevancy to the human situation—here our human strengths and our human weaknesses are manifested; here are the ultimate relevancies of every age revealed; and here, in the midst of great change, we must count on our few reliable anchors, our few tried and true directions, our few bright stars in the blackness of night, whatever the winds of change. This is in the best Catholic tradition and present reality—the ancient wisdom, ever old and ever new. But it must be made to come to life and to shine today for our students. Let us admit that we have not done too well in this department.

Perhaps relevancy is really a state of mind that can be insinuated and inspired by great teachers as one views the Grecian wars, the Roman or Holy Roman Empire, the Renaissance and the Reformation, the Industrial Revolution or the Space Age. All of these human events have something to say about the challenge and response of man to man and to his total global environment, the moral issues, the stretching of man's spirit. All are highly relevant if seen in the total human context. We might add that even the most relevant issues may be taught irrelevantly unless one is sensitive to man, his promise and his fears, his vision and his blindness, his aspirations and his failures.

There is a second issue which today seizes our students—involvement. Again, all is not simple or uncomplicated. All of us who lived through the apathetic generation of the fifties should welcome the desire of this generation to be involved.

Let us admit that here, too, we in Catholic higher education have a strong tradition of paternalism, of deciding everything for our students whatever their own minds in the matter.

This will no longer wash. Not only are we no longer *in loco parentis*, but also neither are their parents. In the present juvenocracy, all wisdom is conferred on youth by age eighteen, with or without the vote. They know what is best for themselves, and the present tendency is to defer to their judgment: on discipline, on regulations in the dormitories, on who shall speak at the college or university, on who shall be punished and how; in addition, they often demand a voice in faculty senates and on boards of trustees.

Obviously, all of these issues are not of equal merit or importance. I would say, as a general principle, that their desire for involvement is good, as it affects their education, their student government, their extracurricular life, their concern that the university be a community in which they have a real and not a fictitious part. I believe that we can establish structures that give them both involvement and voice in all of these matters without instantly conferring upon them the earned competence that should characterize faculty or the ultimate responsibility that is the prerogative of trustees.

We should involve students in every legitimate way to the extent that they are willing to assume responsibility, as well as to assert their rights. The results should ultimately be measured by their growth in maturity, insight, and creativity, and the basic standard should be educational development, the vitality of our institutions, and the greater realization of community on all the layers that characterize the educational enterprise. Also, we must take some chances and have more faith in this younger generation and have more understanding of their concerns.

Student involvement may be a blessing or a curse in our institutions. All our efforts should be bent to make it a blessing, a step forward, a new look that integrates rather than compromises. There is no easy path or instant wisdom in this matter, but I am still in favor of the open mind and the adventurous spirit—provided that we preserve for competence those problems and decisions which demand competence. We can do this and still open up our structures, as never before, for student participation that will be educative for them and for us.

I have a third and last consideration regarding students. If we read the signs of the times, young people today have a very special approach to the ultimate religious reality, which is union with God. We, in our day, realized this by the sacramental approach. They have discovered a new sacrament—service to the poor and the disadvantaged. Why disparage their desires to find in service to others a new form of prayer?

If they find and serve Christ in the hungry, the thirsty, the naked, the imprisoned, the essential has been realized. They find Christ and they serve him, as he himself indicated he might be found and served. This is a more difficult way than that to which we are accustomed, and I suspect that they will soon find that to persevere in this difficult quest they will need new sources of grace and power that are available to them in the mass, the sacraments, and prayer. They may, if they walk this path, find a deeper and a more realistic spirituality than we found. Perhaps they will avoid the dichotomy of the pious person who was totally lacking in a hunger for justice, a compassion for the poor of the world.

Educationally, I believe this means that we must find new and creative outlets for the idealism, generosity, and dedication of this generation of students. If we found no educational problem in giving credit to students who mixed chemicals or measured elements in the laboratory, why find it difficult to give credit to those students who seek a practical outlet for sociological, psychological, economic, or educational theory in their service to those who are the living laboratory, the people who live deprived lives in the cities surrounding our institutions? While I personally have been greatly concerned in turning out graduates who are intellectually competent, I am even more concerned in turning out students who are deeply compassionate. Failing this latter, Catholic institutions of higher learning would with great difficulty justify their special existence, whatever else we do.

Having come this far, I fear I have missed even mentioning

much that should characterize the changing face of Catholic higher education. There is the whole perplexing field of what we are or should be doing for the disadvantaged minorities of America, particularly in light of the special advantages of our own Catholic heritage as a minority that should give us special insights in dealing with other minorities, Catholic or not; the inspiring call to ecumenical endeavor today; the great opportunity for liturgical experimentation, liturgical music and art; the worldwide concern that the word Catholic signifies, as opposed to the chauvinistic, the isolationist, the single culture, namely Western, that engages so much of educational effort today; the use of the freedom that is ours as private institutions for a wide variety of experimentation, especially in philosophical and theological education, that is widely neglected elsewhere in the educational domain and generally done badly by us, too; the establishment of a style of life in our institutions that really reflects the quintessence of a Christian community, united in ideal, study, action, and prayer; the personalism that is our heritage despite its neglect and desiccation on so many of our campuses.

All of these good movements of the spirit are stirring today, and if they are allowed to bloom as they should, I should think that our future survival would not be endangered, but assured, because the world of education needs all of these realities and needs them desperately. Maybe instead of worrying about the changes ahead of us, we should rather decide which changes are needed and overdue, and effect them with vision, vitality, enthusiasm, and verve.

Once again in 1971 I was the keynote speaker for the annual convention of the National Catholic Educational Association, this time in Minneapolis. It had been a wild year—Cambodia had been invaded the previous spring, and students had been killed at Kent State and Jackson State.

In this chapter, I am trying to pinpoint a new focus for Catholic education growing out of an embryonic interpretation of what had been happening in those years. The new focus, really old in the Judeo-Christian Western tradition, is human dignity and all that it means in the life of an individual. Up to this point, I have written mainly on why all this turmoil was taking place. Now, with the help of Ken Keniston, then of Yale, I try to interpret what it really means and what educators might learn from this experience.

At this time, I had been meeting several days each month with Clark Kerr and the distinguished members of the Carnegie Commission on the Future of Higher Education, and the thoughts in this chapter ran through all of our discussions. My task here was to make a meaningful crisis productive for Catholic educators who had been defensive about their task, losing many of their colleagues and institutions, suffering a very real financial crisis in the midst of everything else that was happening.

Again, I was trying to give them a vision of where we might be going, how we might lead the way to a new emphasis in educating the young at a time when young people were hungry for a new challenge and fresh values. I am happy, too, that some of the youthful revolutionaries whom I knew quite well are living good and productive lives today. They did learn something important that stuck with them.

VII

New Focus for Catholic Higher Education in the 1970s

The dignity of man is the most central moral issue of our times. One must note that every aspect of what we called "the youth revolution" stemmed from a new perception of human dignity, a new concern to achieve more dignity and sanctity for human life, more meaning and more rights for all human beings.

If our lives in education have any meaning or significance, it will be in our reading the signs of the times and in educating the young of our times in the visions and values that will civilize and make for reasonable human progress and lasting peace on earth. These visions and values will today inevitably hinge on the dignity of man, the sacredness of human life, the calling of man to greatness, even to the portraying of God's image and likeness in his life. The vision hinges as well on a sense of faith and hope and charity that transcends the travail of the hour or the changes of the moment. Whatever the changes in the theological perception and description of Christianity in our times, there can be no diminution of Catholic education's lifelong commitment to a concept of human life that derives its meaning, purpose, and direction from faith and hope and love of God and man.

The revolution of the young in our time can illuminate and even inspire greater efforts on the part of Catholic educators to make possible in our day a very special contribution to the totality of educational effort around us. We, especially in

Catholic higher education, have over the past two decades been unusually defensive and self-deprecating. That day is over and gone. I have voiced my share of the earlier criticism regarding the academic excellence of Catholic institutions. Now, the key concern is to use this newly acquired competence in the interest of man's dignity and human progress. We must now endow students not only with competence, but also with the compassion and commitment to use their competence in the interest of the less fortunate. While we might have fewer schools and fewer students and fewer faculty, especially religious teachers, in the days to come, the fact is that, given this new dimension, our role has never been more important, more needed, or more welcome.

The whole educational enterprise has fallen upon hard times and is in disrepute among many who view it with scorn or deep concern. Most people think little about the cataclysm of change through which we have passed and are passing. Few have bothered to analyze the movements or the behavior or the concerns of the young. It is too easy to condemn them out of hand, to proffer simplistic solutions that make sense to the elders and dismay their children. We in Catholic education cannot afford the luxury of nonsense or simplistic solutions. We must understand the young and their revolution, and bridge the generation gap between young and old, teacher and taught, adult and adolescent. Personally, I believe that Catholic education on all levels is in a position to profit greatly from such an enterprise, to deepen our efforts and to justify, as never before, our very special kind of educational effort, if it is responsive to the needs of our times and our youth.

Take the issue of war and peace. It is certainly in our tradition that violent solutions are idiotic approaches to the resolution of human problems, that they are only productive of widows and orphans, destruction and ruin, degradation, not civilization. Our educational efforts should be sensitive to every endeavor to foster peace and nonviolence as the greatest values for humans in a world given over to violence, destruction, and war. The first time that Notre Dame offered a class in the nonviolent solution of human problems, 500 students immediately signed up for it and began to make nonviolence a life-style as well as an academic study. Our educational efforts have too often in the past equated patriotism with militarism, rather than stressing the wide spectrum of possible services to our country in nonviolent ways. While our students have often distinguished themselves in the military, I was astounded to find that, while Notre Dame produced more Peace Corps volunteers than any other Catholic university, there were over thirty secular universities—some admittedly much larger—ahead of us in the number of Peace Corps volunteers they produced. All other Catholic universities were way down the line, if they appeared at all, on the list. Incidentally, the list is not classified. You can have it for the asking and it does tell us something about war and peace, and Catholic education, and a fostering and a focus on human dignity through humanitarian efforts.

At this point, one might well consider the words of Father Robert Drinan, the second Catholic priest to be elected to the United States House of Representatives in all our history:

I am afraid that I cannot expect much support from the Catholic community in America in relation to my conviction that the draft should be repealed. Catholic opinion on the subject is probably about the same as that of middle America, or perhaps even more reluctant to eliminate conscription. This state of affairs raises the troubling problem of the failure of communication between church leaders and the laity on the fundamental questions of conscription and war.

The widespread ignorance of Catholics in America regarding traditional Catholic and Christian opposition to military conscription has once again intensified within me the shattering realization that on the primordial moral questions regarding peace in the family of nations, millions of Catholics are morally and theologically illiterate.

Take civil rights, another focus of the youthful revolution.

Here again human dignity is at stake, in education, in housing and neighborhoods, in employment—our institutions included—in the administration of justice, public accommodations, and all the rest. Again, we have, theologically and philosophically, a strong tradition for human dignity and human rights. It should be a keystone of our educational endeavor. But is it? One thinks of the Catholic educated who stoned nuns and priests in Chicago because they were marching for integrated neighborhoods and equal rights for blacks. One thinks of the very few blacks we have educated in our schools (until recently in the inner city) and, even worse, the very few Chicanos who, as Catholics, have had an even closer claim on our apostolic efforts. In my years in the civil rights movement, in and out of government, I have met surprisingly few Catholics, although our schools educate millions annually, presumably in Christian values relevant to the problems of our day. I do receive a surprisingly large number of hate letters from Catholic ethnics every time I put in a good word for blacks or Chicanos.

The young, thank God, largely do not share these ugly prejudices of their elders. Our education should nurture in them this hunger for equality, this respect for the human dignity of every human being, whatever his or her race or color. The young are open to our teaching and example, and we have the wonderful opportunity of reversing past studies which show our students to be singularly undistinguished in their values relating to human equality following years of Catholic education. We also teach by whatever we do, as much as by what we say. After 125 years of existence, Notre Dame had 45 nonacademic minority employees among a total of over 2,000. With a little effort, four years later we had 345. How hollow our words without our actions.

Another concern of today's youth is for the poor and the needy in every human category, including knowledge. The proudest boast I can make for our students is that the vast majority of them are involved in some kind of social action, helping those less fortunate, whatever their need. Should not every Catholic educational establishment say the same: that the majority of its students are learning by doing, that they do indeed serve the poor in every way possible, some of them highly imaginative? Again, we teach human dignity best by serving it where it is most likely to be disregarded, in the poor and abandoned.

I could go on, writing of national priorities as reflected in our national budget, speaking of the eighteen-year-old vote and all that might mean in the campaign for human dignity. Let me say finally a word about sex, not because it is eye-catching or attention-grabbing, but because it does have some relevance, rather large, to human dignity.

We are living in a sex-drenched civilization today. Catholic education has to face this fact among others. Sex is not unimportant, but neither is it all-important, as many magazines, books, and dramas would lead us and our students to believe. By making sex common, cheap, and omnipresent, modern man has made it meaningless. Here is another challenge for Catholic education: to restore sex to its relatively high importance in human life, to clothe it with the human dignity that makes it so much more important than animal sex, to grant it real dignity and importance within the dimensions of the truly human. No easy task, but one worthy of Catholic education in a world steeped in meaningless or prostituted sex.

One could note many other areas that should concern Catholic educators today and tomorrow. They all bear on human dignity and human rights and the sanctity of that life we call human. One could speak of specific concerns, like abortion, marriage, conscientious objection to a specific war, pentecostal enthusiasm, total dedication, monasticism, service abroad in the missions, contemplation and action, and so many others. We have a full bag of concerns in Catholic education and a most exciting life ahead of us.

To give Catholic education on all levels full scope and efficacy in the days ahead, we shall have to be deeply concerned with human dignity and all that this implies in the life and actions of each human being. If this becomes the leitmotif of Catholic education, the deep concern of Catholic educators, I foresee the day that our schools will overflow with students who find in them a true resonance of their deepest concerns. If this happens, our faculty will be overworked but happy, because of the great work they are doing. Whether or not we will at this time be receiving federal aid, we may well be receiving much more: the respect and gratitude of our fellow educators for the unique work that we are doing in the interest and promotion of human dignity in our times. This would indeed be worthy of our faith, consonant with our Christian hope, and faithful to our charity, which, if truly Christian, surpasses all obstacles and overcomes all that would oppose man's being truly man. And, as modern advertisers would say in the jargon of the day, this is what Catholic education is all about.

SECTION THREE

Special Concerns in Higher Education in Modern America

One day, Dr. Julius Stratton, president of the Massachusetts Institute of Technology and a fellow member of the National Science Board, called to ask a favor. "I think I have a problem, Father Ted," he began. "We have the brightest youngsters in the country in our student body. They will be great scientists and engineers, the best in the world. But sometimes I worry about their values. I've introduced a new measure of humanities into the curriculum, but I fear it becomes overshadowed by the obvious excitement of science and technology. Now to the point. Would you come down this June and give them a good talk on values, the importance of being good human beings?"

I said yes and then the trouble began. How do you stress values to budding young scientists and engineers who are riding on the crest of the wave of the future, the best of a group highly respected and cherished in our modern society, happy at being just what they are? I began the essay seven different times and tore up my efforts until I could find a formula that might work, or at least distract them from all that apparent success and adulation.

I stayed with Jay and his lovely wife, Kay, the night before the commencement and tried out the talk on his three delightful daughters, all in their teens and unusually bright, Taffy, Cary, and Lorrie. They said it was okay, but without undue enthusiasm. As so often happens, I was no more sure the next day as to whether it had come off as I wished.

Two summers ago, which was more than ten years later, I was attending a seminar on world development in Aspen, Colorado. One young Iranian computer expert was especially good in the discussion. At the coffee break, I made a point of meeting him. "Oh, I know you," he said, when I introduced myself. "You spoke at my graduation from M.I.T. I can still remember what you said. You gave it to us about real values. I've never forgotten it."

This chapter is a reprise of my thoughts on that occasion.

VIII

Science and Technology in Modern Perspective

Let me ask—and answer—a few questions relating to science and technology in modern perspective.

First question: Are science and technology a blessing or a curse in today's world? May I say that science and technology are in themselves neither a blessing nor a curse, although, in fact, they are a bit of both and may be either depending upon how they are actually used. Science and technology are in themselves neutral, neither good nor bad. Most simply, they represent two great realities: knowledge and power. Insofar as one becomes competent in science and technology, one possesses this knowledge and this power. It can be used or abused, as can all other forms of knowledge and power. Herein lies the true meaning of science and technology as a blessing or a curse in our day. It is not the quality of our science and technology that really answers this first question, but the quality of our scientists and engineers, *as persons*. It is mainly persons who give a moral quality to things, who bless or curse, who do good or evil, with the means available.

Second question: Are science and technology the greatest forms of knowledge and power in the world today? Science is knowledge of the physical world, of those things which are sensibly observable, or measurable, capable of being conceptualized in mathematical formulae, submitted to hypothesis and verification. The power of science and technology is physical power, awesome, yes, if seen internally as fission or fusion in the heart of the atom, or externally in the brilliance of a supernova. One can well respect and reverence this knowledge and this power. Science and technology represent the really obvious new frontier in our day, they command and fashion most of our resources, they man our front-line defenses, they produce the affluent society, they attract the majority of our most brilliant people, they spark the revolution of rising expectations around the world.

One can say all of this and yet not admit that science and technology are the greatest forms of knowledge and power in our day. To disagree, one need only believe that there are realities that transcend the physical order. If one says this, he also says that there are limitations to knowledge and power of a physical order, that indeed this knowledge and power need something outside and beyond themselves for their true meaning and direction in the total life of mankind. This proposition was stated very simply ages ago. I cannot improve on this statement: man does not live by bread alone.

In saying this one need not denigrate science and technology. It is not a question of either-or, but of both-and. It is a matter of proportion, of total meaning. Man does need bread, too.

Third question: In view of the foregoing, are science and technology overemphasized in the world today? I am not for less science and technology, but more. However, this "more" must be qualified. It is not necessarily more of the same. I will agree that in our own country we have, thanks to science and technology, created the highest standard of living yet known to mankind: better food, better housing, better clothing, better communications and transportation, better medicine, and better life expectancy. Is this bad? Of course not. But it is not automatically good, either. We have spoken here of material benefits—and these alone do not make the life of man good. The worst gangster may enjoy a ranch house, air conditioning, good food and drink, a Cadillac, a private airplane, the best medical care that money can buy, and a long life, too.

When I say more science and technology, I am not thinking of more luxurious living conditions for Americans of every and any quality. I am thinking of the broader context of the world, in which never before have so many millions of people been more poorly housed, or fed, or clothed. Never before have there been more illiterates, more infant deaths, or more people with frustrated hopes for a better life. More science and technology may indeed have an answer for all of these very real human problems, but the answers will only come if scientists and engineers put their science and technology to work in the true service of mankind everywhere, responding to real human needs rather than pampering imagined wants, piling luxury upon luxury, and convenience upon convenience.

Personally, I am not interested in better dog food when people are hungry. I spoke earlier of proportion. Even in the material order, proportion plays an important role. I have seen people dying on the streets of Calcutta; I have seen hungry refugee children on the sampans and in the shacks of Hong Kong; I have seen unnecessary disease in Uganda, in Pakistan, in Brazil and Chile. I have sensed the hopelessness of many of the 900 million illiterates of this world. Against this background, I am slightly nauseated when I see science and technology dedicated to trivial purposes like better deodorants and better detergents, better cosmetics and more aesthetic telephones, better garden sprinklers and better remote control of wrestling and horse operas on television. If this is the overemphasis spoken of, of course we have too much, but how can this knowledge and power be overemphasized if it is directed against man's ancient enemies—hunger, disease, illness, and ignorance? In a world largely frustrated, we cannot be against that which brings great hope.

It is not really science and technology we speak of, but the forces that motivate their use for trivial or meaningful purposes in our day. And again, we speak of a personal equation, of the inner values that lead a scientist or engineer to use his knowledge and his power for noble or trivial ends. The trivial use of science and technology may mean a great personal profit to the scientist or engineer; the noble is rarely profitable.

But this is only to say again that there is indeed a higher order of values that makes science and technology meaningful, and that these values reside not in science and technology, but in the person of the scientist or engineer. He alone confers human nobility upon his knowledge and his power. With highly motivated and dedicated scientists and engineers, the knowledge and power of science and technology will always be a blessing to mankind; indeed, in our day, they may help create a physical situation in which human dignity can finally flower all around the world. But in the hands of those to whom knowledge is a means of personal selfish profit, and power a raw edge for creating fear of utter destruction and conquest of the world to slavery, science and technology can well become a curse. In any event, man makes the difference, for man alone of God's creatures is free to reproduce beauty, order, and justice in this world—or ugliness, disorder, and grinding injustice. Science and technology are powerful means to either purpose. In a free world, it is man, the scientist or engineer, who makes the choice of goals for science and technology in our day.

Fourth question: Wouldn't the world really be a better place if we could replace the current leadership—the politicians, the philosophers, the lawyers, the humanists, and the theologians—with scientists and engineers? I am sure that this question, on the surface, sounds somewhat preposterous, but there are scientists who do profess to have an answer for everything, who have been disillusioned by political and legal forces in our day, who often feel unduly inhibited by philosophy and theology, who legitimately bristle when they are portrayed by the humanists as the new savages, bringing the world to the brink of destruction.

One might make the point that these others, the nonscientists, acted mighty selfish themselves when they had their day of ascendency. I must resort to some oversimplification here, but I think the main point at issue will be evident to you. The Greeks in their day reduced all knowledge to philosophy: a remnant of this remains, as many scientists today receive Ph.D.'s—doctorates of philosophy. The Romans brought our civilization a heritage of law and political order. Many of our current legal principles were formulated long ago in the Code of Justinian, when science was fairly primitive. Renaissance man almost worshiped the arts. Science was simply a liberal art in those days. In medieval times, theological synthesis was in highest vogue. The earliest universities turned round about the faculty of theology. The queen of the sciences was theology's most cherished title. No scientist or engineer would have had then the ascendency each enjoys today. In fact, the explosive beginnings of science and technology were most often met with resistance and misunderstanding.

Would it be any surprise then if history were to repeat itself, if those who hold the ascendency today were to claim as their exclusive rights the center of the stage, as the philosophers, the lawyers, the humanists, and the theologians did in their day? Would it be incomprehensible if scientists and engineers were to claim today that they, with their revolutionary new knowledge and power, could do a better job of running the world than those who preceded them in man's long history of intellectual development? I grant you that the temptation is there, and very real. There is historical precedent for those who would answer my latest question in the affirmative and claim exclusive leadership today for scientists and engineers as the best the world may expect and need.

I could readily understand this stance, but again, in disagreeing with this position, I would only underline one perceptive statement: that those who are merely children of their day, who do not understand history, condemn themselves to repeat all the human errors of the past. I have commented amply on the modern world's need for science and technology, but have always reiterated the need for other values if this new knowledge and power are not to be perverted in our day, to man's great loss—indeed, possibly to his utter destruction. I have no argument against enthusiasm and zeal for science and technology—indeed I share it with a great and abiding new hope. But man does have other needs. There are other legitimate and very important areas of knowledge and power, and frankly some of them are ultimately much more important to man than science and technology. Science and technology cannot have their true human meaning and direction without reference to this total world of the human spirit.

What is really needed today is not exclusivity of knowledge, but a deeper unity of all knowledge, past, present, and yet to come. Each kind of knowledge—scientific, humanistic, philosophical, and theological—has its proper sphere, its proper method of learning and knowing, its innate limitations, too. And each kind of knowledge bears some relation to man's nature and destiny, some service to offer to man and to the God who made man to know, to love, and to be happy in the knowledge of all that is true, and in the love of all that is beautiful and good.

It is true that man's intellectual history up to now has represented a long series of abortive efforts to establish an unwarranted hegemony for this or that kind of knowledge. In our day, you who represent that which is best in science and technology have the unique opportunity of changing this unhealthy historical trend. I cannot imagine this happening in our day unless you possess some deep conviction to see that it does happen, especially in your own intellectual and professional life. It is most probably you who must take the lead in becoming humanists, jurists, philosophers, yes, theologians, too. We must begin to repeat with Terence: nothing human is alien to me; no human insight, no human misery, no human beauty, no human knowledge, no human anguish, no human value, no human hunger. Anything less than this leads to a truncated or sterile life, a life without fullest meaning and direction and depth.

It is meaningless and futile, for example, to labor for better communications without being interested and concerned about what is being communicated, to make abundance of food available in one corner of the world for storage while countless millions go hungry, to make quantum advances in the speed of transportation without ever asking yourselves: why am I here and where am I going? All of these questions and concerns relate not to the quality of things, but to the quality of persons. Any person, whatever his talent or skill or competence, who does not seek wise answers to these broader human questions, is unfit for significant leadership in human affairs. He is at best an anchorless manipulator, at worst a menace.

Last question: What are our values? Each of us must make up our own list, of course, but here are some suggestions of enduring values, those that share the patina of eternity.

Commitment to truth in all its forms: the joy of ever seeking truth, the peace of finding truth everywhere, the courage of living truth always. Open-mindedness is the prelude to this commitment, intellectual honesty is its truest spirit, and purity of life is essential to both possession of the truth and commitment to what it demands of us.

Commitment to what is good and excellent. I mean here no narrowly selfish good, but that every good and noble inspiration might find in us a champion and a defender, and indeed a personification. What is good for our own moral integrity, yes, but also the realization that we will often find ourselves and our good in spending ourselves and our talent for the good of others who need us. To avoid the taint of intellectual and moral mediocrity; to be willing to stand for something, even something unpopular, if it is good; to be willing to be a minority of one if needs be—this is part of the commitment. But not to be a neutral where principle is involved, a moral cipher, a pragmatic compromiser who easily takes on the protective coloration of whatever moral environment happens to be at hand, this also is ruled out by commitment. Is it too much to expect of you? Anything less is all too little.

A passion for justice in our times. Again, not merely justice for ourselves, or our families, or our professions, but especially a passion for justice as regards those who have few friends and fewer champions. There are great and festering injustices in our country and in our world. We can sidestep them if we wish; we can close our eyes and say it is none of our business. But remember that freedom and equality of opportunity in our times are quite indivisible. If one class, or nation, or race of men is not really free, then the freedom of all men is endangered. Injustice breeds more injustice, disorder begets more disorder. One does not need a suit of armor, or a white horse, or a sword, but just a sensitivity to justice wherever it is endangered, a quiet passion to be concerned for justice in our times, a compassion for all men who suffer injustice, or the fruits of injustice. Why suggest this to scientists and engineers? Indeed, why not?

Lastly, I would suggest a value that could have many names, but the simplest name of all is *faith*. Faith is not an easy virtue for scientists and engineers, who in their own professions instinctively take nothing on faith. But in the broader world of man's total voyage through time to eternity, faith is not only a gracious companion, but an essential guide. Let us face the matter frontally and in its deepest dimensions. Faith begins with belief in God, he who is, the ultimate eternal source of all else that is: all truth, all goodness, all beauty, all justice, all order. Science, as science, tells us nothing of this, nor does science deny any of this, unless you take seriously the prattling of cosmonaut Titov about not seeing God while in orbit.

On the other hand, one should observe, as Whitehead did, that the world of faith is not uncongenial to science. God is not only a God of omnipotence and freedom, but also a God of rationality and order. While he was free to create or not create a cosmos, and in choosing to create was free to create this cosmos or some other, when he did create it was a cosmos and not a chaos that was created, since it had to reflect his own perfection.

Because God is rational, his work is orderly, and because he is free, there is no predicting absolutely just what that precise order will be. The world of faith is then a world congenial to empirical science with its twin method of observation and experiment. Unless there were regularities in the world, there would be nothing for science to discover, and being contingent regularities, they must be open to hypothesis and verified by experimentation. This is the rhythm of modern physics: experimental expansion and theoretical development. As an aside, may I express in passing the hope that the theoretical physicists will soon bring some order out of the present chaos of subatomic particles. I am sure there is more to this than we now know.

Every year in Vienna, at the Atoms for Peace Conference, I

have to assure my Russian scientist friends that I do indeed believe in God and that this does not preclude my believing in science, too—for entirely different reasons, but without becoming schizophrenic about it either. Much would be gained, I believe, if the scientists and engineers in our day were men of faith as well as men of science. Too long has there been an imagined chasm between the very real values of the physical and spiritual worlds. Faith I take to be a gift of God, but one that is amenable to rational foundations and prayerful preparation. It is rather a luminous opening on another world, that adds new personal dimensions to one's life and wider vistas to one's highest endeavors, in science or in any other field of intellectual interest. For these reasons, I have added faith to my list of the values that make life more meaningful.

During Detlev Bronk's tenure as chairman of the National Science Board, he asked me to chair a committee of the board to resolve what was then a troublesome question: whether or not the National Science Foundation should support the social sciences. Most of the board members took a dim view of this, as they were mostly physical or natural scientists who did not want to see the then fairly meager educational and research funds diverted from their fields.

Det gave me a committee that was so evenly split that I had to decide the outcome with my vote. The committee report, advising support for the social sciences, came to the board during a late summer meeting when I had to be in Africa. It also came at the end of a long and difficult day when the board was feeling testy. They simply rejected the report, and that would have been that, except that Det Bronk said, "You can't reject a report when the chairman isn't here to defend it, so we'll vote again in October." When I returned, Det called and warned me of almost certain defeat for the report in the next meeting.

I came expecting the worst, made a strong presentation of the committee's report, stressing the growing importance of the social sciences to the nation. To my surprise, they approved the report, including the establishment of a Social Science Office which would soon become a division of the foundation and which is now allocating about $20 million a year to social science.

I mention all of this because it may appear that I am unusually difficult with the social scientists in the chapter that follows. I wrote as a friend, and friends should be honest with each other. President Harlan Hatcher of the University of Michigan asked if I would speak on the occasion of the dedication of their new Institute for Social Research in 1966. I remarked that they might not like what I thought I should say. "Don't worry about that," he commented. "You know that universities are made up of people who think otherwise so why shouldn't you be free to challenge them?" So I did. As the last chapter tried to find the value dimension for physical and natural scientists and engineers, here I try to do the same for social scientists. (Incidentally, to demonstrate how times change and the wheel turns, the new director of the National Science Foundation is, for the first time, a social scientist, Dr. Richard C. Atkinson.)

IX

Social Science in an Age of Social Revolution

A popular cultural history of the great ages of Western civilization characterizes the early and late Middle Ages as the Age of Faith, followed by the Romantic Renaissance, the Reformation, the Age of Reason, the Enlightenment, the Age of Political Revolution, and, for the better part of the last century, increasingly in this century, the Age of Social Revolution. One could chart various ages of human knowledge the same way, without perfect overlap, but with some convergence. I believe that one might, without too great danger of oversimplification, say that the ages of faith were a golden age for theological knowledge, and that our age of social revolution has seen not only the birth in most cases, but also the flowering of the various social sciences.

No human knowledge exists or develops in a vacuum. It is the total ambient of man's culture and concern that is inviting or negating as regards the development of specialized human knowledges. The action is really an interaction once it begins, with man's new knowledge affecting his culture just as his culture in a given age invites and nourishes the new knowledge. We take this for granted when we observe how the industrial revolution encouraged and was in turn nurtured by a new technology, or see the interaction between the advent of a nuclear and space age and the rapid development of a wide range of new sciences and technologies that make this age so spectacular in its achievements. One other observation is important here, if we can assume that history repeats itself: the curves of new advances, both in culture and in knowledge, are not merely linear, but exponential. We have come, even in a matter of common speech, to describe modern developments as explosions—the knowledge explosion, the population explosion. Culture and knowledge together are given to quantum jumps along new lines, even though one must always keep in perspective the agelong glacial movement of the total worldwide evolutionary process in culture and knowledge. One can also note historically that it is no simple matter to correlate the new quantum jumps with the totality of knowledge and culture existing at the moment of the explosive new advance. Faith in the old is shaken, institutions sometimes collapse, tradition is battered by new winds and waves of gale proportions, and the weaker souls totally and exclusively embrace the new as if man had known nothing before. The new gain is often enough ambiguous in the face of the old loss.

Against this admittedly sketchy background, how do we relate the explosive growth of the social sciences within an explosive age of social revolution? I am prepared to assume that they are related in some way, although I am far from assuming that they are in fact related as fruitfully or as positively as they should be, or as fully, for example, as the new sciences and technologies are related to the nuclear and space age that is also in process today. The relationship of the social sciences to the age of social revolution is by no means as obvious a relationship as that enjoyed by the physical sciences, but in the long run of man's history the relationship of the social sciences to social revolution may well be ultimately much more important than the relation of the physical sciences to the space age.

The 1965 investigation of the National Science Foundation by the Daddario Committee of the House showed a more than casual concern for the development of the social sciences, even within the National Science Foundation. Why? Again we perceive the interwoven fabric of the social structure. There probably would not be an age of social revolution without all of the new human opportunities made possible by the new sciences and technologies. On the other hand, the very existence of these new opportunities, whatever widespread human hopes they inspire, is no guarantee that most of mankind will indeed see these hopes realized in their lives. A great society might be postponed by a costly war. A world on the brink of development may see its means of development, both human and financial, moving mostly in another direction, for example, into the void of space. The spectacular may displace the pedestrian, even though, ultimately, pedestrian hopes for food and shelter and health and education are humanly more important. One might speculate as to whether Egyptian society might have had a longer life and a deeper influence if social justice had been chosen as its best goal instead of pyramids and monumental statuary to mark the tombs of past greatness. In any event, the empire declined relatively soon after the building of Abu Simbel.

No culture has an infinity of talent or energy—not even ours. I suspect that latent in the Daddario Committee's concern was the thought that somehow, in the complex interrelationships that characterize modern society, the presence of a stronger social science, or more correctly, of more articulate social scientists, might influence our nuclear and space age, as well as the whole broad world of social revolution in which we live.

At this point, I am perfectly conscious of the fact that I am opening the proverbial can of worms. But I do so because I am convinced that while a cultural context may inspire a whole new set of human knowledges, such as the social sciences, these cannot grow and develop as they should unless they in turn are relevant to the problems that brought them into being. This may seem to be an excessively pragmatic point of view, but I believe it reflects the reality of the situation without excluding other intellectual values inherent in the social sciences themselves.

Here we face a dilemma of monumental proportions, indeed a crossroads where the turning one way or another may signal the ultimate fruitfulness or the ultimate demise of the social sciences in the context of modern culture. I realize that the immediate challenge and response is not quite so black and white, but again, ultimately, the dilemma is very real and must, I think, be faced in all frankness.

The social sciences are mainly parvenus among the sciences. They came upon a field already largely dominated by the physical and natural sciences. It is human and understandable that, in an effort to be comfortable in already occupied territory, the newcomers took on the protective coloration of the place and times, adopting the reigning regime's proudest title of science—as if this were the only source of respectability and pride—and adopting the title of science in an altogether too univocal sense.

There followed many other understandable developments: the amassing of data for the sake of data, the attempt to quantify the unquantifiable, the cult of mathematical verification in an effort to establish theories ultimately beyond mathematics, the worship of objectivity to an extent that often sterilized what might have been very fruitful research, the confusion between counting heads and establishing what are essentially philosophical norms, the blurring of what is average and what is truly significant, the development of so-called scientific terminology and occult nomenclature that allowed an esoteric statement of obvious fact to masquerade as scientific wisdom when it was in fact not only not worth stating, but also stated in murky and turgid rhetoric. Regarding this latter point, may I say that the inability to communicate signals the end of usefulness for any element in a culture, be it religion, art, or science.

This is obviously an overstatement of some of the reasons why the general public, as well as the physical and natural scientists, refused to take much of early social science seriously. In attempting to be something it never can be, social science has at times prevented itself from performing the very task it can and must perform to survive, to develop, and to be useful to the age that brought it forth and needs its strong assistance. Social sciences, it seems to me as an *auslander*, need desperately to find their own identities, to elaborate their proper fields of inquiry and their proper methods, and, I will add, all the social sciences need desperately to develop fruitful relationships with other human knowledges and other methods of knowing, without ceasing to be their own valid, honest, useful, and respectable selves. It is dangerous to categorize, *in globo*, all the social sciences, but I am willing to concede that my judgments weigh more heavily against some of the social sciences than others.

Perhaps I can best illustrate what I am trying to say here by citing an example from a field in which social science should have had great effect, but, in fact, did have precious little effect for many years: civil rights. This despite the fact that it was for more than a century a problem central to the age of social revolution.

After about eighty years with no civil rights federal legislation, our Congress, after a long and involved filibuster, finally enacted the Civil Rights Act of 1957. It became perfectly obvious during the discussion that there was a great dearth of simple factual information about the problem, and because of this, all suggested legislative solutions were viewed with distrust and suspicion. Consequently, a great portion of the 1957 act was devoted to the establishment of a six-man, bipartisan federal commission to acquire the facts, to assess them in light of the existing laws, and to make specific recommendations to the president and the Congress.

Eight years and many volumes later, about 80 percent of all the commission's recommendations have been enacted into federal law. How did this happen? First of all, the enabling legislation only spoke specifically of studying voting, but after some filibustering within the commission (we, the members, were also evenly split North and South), we early decided to study education and housing, as well as voting. Two years later, after many hearings, investigations, and the publication of our first 1959 report, it was decided to move into the additional fields of employment and administration of justice. Thus, our 1961 report covered a factual analysis of five fields in five volumes. The success of this approach would not have been possible if we had not decided from the start to make some value judgments (and they were far from obvious at the time, not to mention their being very unpopular). The most fundamental of these judgments diagnosed the organic nature of the problem and its ultimate solution, the interrelationship of voting and education, education and employment, employment and housing, and the effect of all of these together upon how a minority achieves equality of opportunity and justice under the law. We needed more than census data because the census did not ask the right questions. We needed data that was beyond reproach, given the emotional overtones of the total problem and the number of anxious congressmen and senators looking over our shoulders. Whatever one says about objectivity, there has not been substantiated a single factual misstatement in any of our growing library of special studies and general reports.

However, even given the proper data, I do not believe that much would have come of it had we not been willing to assess it vigorously with all the total wisdom and courage at our commission's command. This meant more value judgments of a growing complexity from an economic, social, political, psychological, anthropological, cultural point of view. We had to announce these judgments in clear yet firm words, not editorializing on the one hand, nor hiding behind murky prose on the other, or tergiversating because we knew the president and the Congress might well not take kindly to our judgments. Indeed, they often did not, and a president's broadside was laid upon us for even suggesting the withholding of federal funds, which eventually became Title VI of the 1964 Civil Rights Act.

Someone might object at this point by saying that we commissioners were not really social scientists, even though working in a germane field, and that, therefore, we did not have professional reputations to uphold by being completely nonnormative. Before responding to this, may I recall a scholar named Gunnar Myrdal, who seemed to have lacked similar inhibitions and yet stands out with very few others like a giant among the pygmies for all previous work done in this field.

Even so, the objection is worthy of more than an ad hominem response. Let me say quite bluntly that I believe all important social science problems are pregnant with values, for the simple reason that the objects of social science study, man, his culture, his institutions, his processes, are all something of value or not worth studying. What man is and what his institutions are can be something of more or less value. Understanding of man and his culture and his institutions can be very valuable or worthless if all is misunderstood. Solutions can be valuable if they follow deep understanding of the relevant facts, or without value if they look at irrelevant facts with blind judgment. The very statement of a social science problem represents something valuable or worthless. The process of investigating a social science problem represents something worthwhile or useless; and the conclusions resulting are something of value or not, depending on a whole series of real value judgments all along the line of research. To say then that the social scientist is not interested in values is, to me at least, nonsense. Without values there is no science, no discernment, no judgment, no relevance, and certainly no meaningful relationship between social science and the age of social revolution in which we live. Also, without values, there are no institutions, since all institutions represent organization to do something worthwhile.

Maybe the easiest shortcut to an answer is to focus on the question, Social revolution for what?—as Robert Lynd did many years ago in his book, *Knowledge For What?* I know of no more substantive answer to this question than to consider, at more length than is possible here, the fundamental dignity of the human person. While this involves philosophical and theological considerations outside the realm of social science itself, I know of no valid reason why the social scientist cannot also be a philosopher or a theologian, or both, if this exercise will enrich his primary intellectual endeavor in social science, particularly as regards its most central and complex focus: the human person.

Listen for a moment to what one lay philosopher-theologian has to say about that most indefinable of oft-defined realities, the human person. I quote from Jacques Maritain's *Principes d'une Politique Humaniste*.

What do we mean precisely when we speak of the human person? When we say that a man is a person, we do not mean merely that he is an individual, in the sense that an atom, a blade of grass, a fly or an elephant is an individual.

Man is an individual who holds himself in hand by intelligence and will. He does not exist only in a physical manner. He has a spiritual super-existence through knowledge and love; he is, in a way, a universe in himself, a microcosm, in which the great universe in its entirety can be encompassed through knowledge; and through love, he can give himself completely to beings who are to him, as it were, other selves, a relation for which no equivalent can be found in the physical world. The human person possesses these characteristics because in the last analysis man, this flesh and these perishable bones which are animated and activated by a divine fire, exists "from the womb to the grave" by virtue of the very existence of his soul, which dominates time and death. Spirit is the root of personality. The notion of personality thus involves that of totality and independence; no matter how poor and crushed he may be, a person, as such, is a whole and subsists in an independent manner. To say that man is a person is to say that in the depths of his being he is more than a part, and more independent than servile. It is to say that he is a minute fragment of matter that is at the same time a universe, a beggar who communicates with absolute being, mortal flesh whose value is eternal, a bit of straw into which heaven enters. It is this metaphysical mystery that religious thought points to when it says that the person is the image of God. The value of the person, his dignity and his rights belong to the order of things naturally sacred which bear the imprint of the Father of being, and which have in Him the end of their movement.

If this means anything, it means that of all valuable things on earth, man is most valuable because he is an end, not a means. The revolution today is for him, that his dignity might at long last be realized on earth, as well as in heaven, that no matter what his race, his color, his country, his culture, or his religion or the lack of it, he is a *res sacra*, a sacred thing, a person who deserves better of this world if his inner dignity is not to be lost in the outer indignity of so much that is utterly inhuman in modern life. This is what the social revolution is all about. It is a revolution for human equality, for human development, for an end to the poverty, the hunger, the illness, the ignorance, the homelessness, the utter hopelessness that afflict so many human persons today. I assume we agree that all of this is worthwhile, of value, because the human person is of all earthly realities the most valuable. And I continue to assume that if social science is to be relevant to this age of social revolution it must become more and more involved in what the social revolution is all about.

I would like to conclude with a series of propositions that round out my basic theme. While these points are strongly normative, I do not intend that they be doctrinaire, or indicate any more than one man's opinion as to what is central to the vitality and development of the social sciences in our day. You may, if you wish, say that like most free advice, these six points are worth what they cost.

1. The dignity of every individual human person is of the highest importance to all of the social sciences. This reality is most important in the choice and relevance of social science studies, and provides a framework within which the scientific study proper to the social sciences does not degenerate into a scientism only proper to the physical and natural sciences. The mathematical and statistical are often thwarted by the human freedom which is the glory and the risk of the human person. Mathematical methods are a legitimate means to reach an end, if molecules and men are not confused. The average may indicate something about Stratford-on-Avon and completely miss Shakespeare in the process. Moreover, the purposes of the social sciences are not merely detached scientific exercises, but representative of the hopes, the achievements, and, alas, also the aberrations of the human person at its best and worst. In this, the social sciences are more akin to the novel and drama than to computer and laboratory technologies, for the totality of the social sciences are attempting to understand, chapter and verse, on visible evidence, the most complex, sacred, and perverse of all realities, the human person and the ambiguities of human life, human culture, human institutions and processes.

2. Social scientists today should show concern, even com-

passion, for the subjects they study. I have indicated above that the dispassion of most social scientists for many years in the face of the civil rights problem did them no honor. Social scientists are forfeiting their highest privilege when they approach man in the same manner as a physicist studying the activity of high energy particles or a chemist investigating electron paramagnetic resonance. Even in the achievement of great power, Einstein worked mightily for peace, and after Hiroshima and Nagasaki, Oppenheimer said that the scientist now knew sin.

The hypotheses of the social scientist should be relevant to the real, critical, and urgent human problems of our day. His experimentation is the more difficult because human problems are more complex than physical, chemical, or biological problems, but nonetheless, the reasonable and rigorous testing of social science hypotheses is no less enlightening and much more important. Man lives and grows daily on moral rather than mathematical certitudes.

3. The social sciences are central to the age of social revolution, which gave them birth and a great field for development. A suitable response to this challenge would be a real contribution of the social sciences to the purposes of these new revolutionary movements towards a greater human equality and a greater human development in our day. Building economic models may be great mathematical fun, but rather useless if they are completely unrelated to the economic facts of life in the underdeveloped countries. Learning research is sterile if it is never related to the third of mankind that is illiterate, either actually or functionally. Interpersonal relations studies are fine, but better if applied to the second revolution in civil rights, the formation of individual as compared to national conscience in the matter, or family disintegration, or administrative-faculty-student tensions, or the exciting new ecumenical perspectives for understanding between religions and cultures, or the ever-latent tensions of cold-war realities.

4. The social scientist may still be detached and reserved regarding the normative or value content of his studies, but as a human person, in touch with other fields of knowledge that supplement and buttress his studies, he cannot forever sit on

the fence. What I am saying, hopefully, loudly, and clearly, is that concern on the part of the social scientist as a person should in some measure be followed by commitment. David Riesman is not afraid to come out foursquare for the Peace Corps as an antidote to the fatheadedness of our times. He says it more elegantly, but there it is. Tocqueville has had more influence than most valueless, judgment-free political scientists, and Michael Harrington has had an influence denied to those who are factually perfect, but sterile in values and judgments based on values. The social scientist is an informed member of the human race. He should be heard on the controverted issues of our times. He has much to add to the dialogue that would be a powerful corrective to the voice of prejudice, ignorance, and myth. He should be an active member of the club in the formulation of public policy. He should have his considered convictions and clearly express them in understandable language. Otherwise, he will be reduced to a self-conscious conversation, with all the appropriate jargon, addressed only to other social scientists and lost to the public discussions that guide our policy and our culture, not to mention our prevalent values, which will be the poorer for his nonparticipation.

5. Much the same as the physical scientists and technologists of our age, the social scientist must resist the seduction of the grants and subsidies available to him. He alone should decide the direction and orientation of his own research. Here is the great value of social science in the university context. It may still say yes or no, and be the captain of its own destiny. Prostitution is an ancient art and the oldest profession. The social scientist is not immune to its call unless he adds integrity and conviction to his special art and to his high challenge in our times. Freedom of ideas, freedom of research and study—these are still the highest and most productive calls.

6. As a paradigm of the above, I refer you to Barbara Ward's latest works on economic development. She says clearly and with style that which her best social science judgment recommends. She casts it upon the open market for discussion. She has no illusions of infallibility and does not indulge in nationalistic or selfish concerns. She just says what seems to

make sense, in view of the evidence, and it does. If someone knows better, or has better evidence, he is free to gainsay her. But just in speaking this way, she makes a great contribution and sets an example that I trust may be personally more convincing than my words.

The social sciences, with all the scholarly resources available to them, have the task of promoting in our times the full depths and heights of human dignity—that which we cherish for ourselves and may make possible increasingly for others less fortunate.

Towards the end of 1973, the education editor of the *New York Times* called me to say that after he had most of his year's-end educational supplement finished, it occurred to him that he had nothing on values, which was then becoming more and more a concern for both educators and the general public. All of the young White House men involved in Watergate were products of some of our best educational institutions. They were obviously competent people; after all, they manipulated a stunning victory for Mr. Nixon. Yet, by their own admission, many of them confessed that they had not learned to ask the right questions, such as, "Is this the right thing do do? Is it honest, just, or fair?" They made ends of means, substance of shadow, rights of wrongs. In a word, they were hucksters.

Curiously, higher education is today being asked to concern itself with values, at a time when vocational education—learning how to *do* something—is being on many sides preferred over liberal education—learning how to *be* somebody worthwhile. There is no way of learning values apart from the liberal arts and sciences. Learning values has always been a difficult task. Without liberal education, it is an impossible task.

I believe that every university student should learn how to do something well, by way of getting his or her foot in the job door following graduation. But once inside, the quality of the person, how he or she thinks, speaks, judges, decides, and *is*, will largely determine how successful one is, not to mention how happy. The worst that education can do is to fit a youngster in a narrow mold from which there is no upward or lateral mobility. That is the quintessential rut. Education should liberate us from that fate, not consign us to it.

I have been heartened by the reawakening of interest in values. As it affects higher education, I am doubly heartened because it must involve a new concern for better liberal education, too.

X

The Moral Purpose of Higher Education

Somewhere, in that vague morass of rhetoric that has always characterized descriptions of liberal education, one always finds a mention of values. The true purists insist on intellectual values, but there have always been educators, particularly among founders of small liberal arts colleges in the nineteenth century, who likewise stressed moral values as one of the finest fruits of their educational process, especially if their colleges were inspired by a religious group.

I believe it to be a fairly obvious fact that we have come full circle in our secularized times. Today one hears all too little of intellectual values, and moral values seem to have become a lost cause in the educational process. I know educators of some renown who practically tell their students, "We don't care what you do around here as long as you do it quietly, avoid blatant scandal, and don't give the institution a bad name."

Part of this attitude is an overreaction to *in loco parentis*, which goes from eschewing responsibility for students' lives to just not caring how they live. It is assumed that how students live has no relation to their education, which is, in this view, solely an intellectual process. Those who espouse this view would not necessarily deny that values are important in life. They just do not think that values form part of the higher education endeavor—if, indeed, they can be taught anyway.

Moral abdication or valuelessness seems to have become a sign of the times. One might well describe the illness of modern society and its schooling as anomie, a rootlessness.

I would like to say right out that I do not consider this to be progress, however modern and stylish it might be. The Greeks (not the fraternities!) were at their best when they insisted that excellence (*arete*) was at the heart of human activity at its noblest, certainly at the heart of education at its civilized best. John Gardner wrote a book on the subject which will best be remembered by his trenchant phrase: "Unless our philosophers and plumbers are committed to excellence, neither our pipes nor our arguments will hold water."

Do values really count in a liberal education? They have to count if you take the word "liberal" at its face value. To be liberal, an education must somehow liberate a person actually to be what every person potentially is: free. Free to be and free to do. What?

Excuse me for making a list, but it is important. The first fruit of a liberal education is to free a person from ignorance, which fundamentally means freedom to think, clearly and logically. Moreover, allied with this release from stupidity—nonthinking or poor thinking—is the freedom to communicate one's thoughts, preferably with clarity, style, and grace, certainly with more than the Neanderthal grunt. A liberal education should also enable a person to judge, which in itself presupposes the ability to evaluate: to prefer this to that, to say this is good and that is bad or, at least, this is better than that. To evaluate is to prefer, to discriminate, to choose, and each of these actions presupposes a sense of values. Liberal education should also enable a person to situate himself or herself within a given culture, religion, race, sex, and to appreciate what is valuable in the given situation, even as simple an evaluation as "black is beautiful." This, too, is a value judgment and a liberation from valuelessness, insecurity, and despair at times. Liberal education, by all of these value-laden processes, should confer a sense of peace, confidence, and assurance on the person thus educated and liberate him or her from the adriftness that characterizes so many in an age of anomie.

Lastly, a liberal education should enable a person to humanize everything that he or she touches in life, which is to say that one is enabled not only to evaluate what one is or does, but that, in addition, one adds value consciously to relationships that might otherwise be banal or superficial or meaningless: relations to God, to one's fellow men, to one's wife or husband or children, to one's associates, one's neighborhood, one's country and world.

In this way, the list of what one expects of liberal education is really a list of the very real values that alone can liberate a person from very real evils or nonvalues—stupidity, meaninglessness, inhumanity.

One might well ask at this juncture, "How are these values attained educationally?" Again, one is almost forced to make a list. Language and mathematics stress clarity, precision, and style if well taught; literature gives an insight into that vast human arena of good and evil, love and hate, peace and violence as real living human options. History gives a vital record of mankind's success and failure, hopes and fears, the heights and the depths of human endeavors pursued with either heroism or depravity—but always depicting real virtue or the lack of it. Music and art purvey a sense of beauty seen or heard, a value to be preferred to ugliness or cacophony. The physical sciences are a symphony of world order, so often unsuccessfully sought by law, but already achieved by creation, a model challenging man's freedom and creativity. The social sciences show man at work, theoretically and practically, creating his world. Too often, social scientists in their quest for a physical scientist's objectivity underrate the influence of freedom—for good or for evil. While a social scientist must remain objective within the givens of his observable data, his best contribution comes when he invokes the values that make the data more meaningful, as Tocqueville does in commenting on the values of democracy in America, Barbara Ward in outlining the value of social justice in a very unjust world, Michael Harrington in commenting on the nonvalue of property. Again, it is the value judgments that ultimately bring the social sciences to life and make them more meaningful in liberating those who study them in the course of a liberal education.

One might ask where the physical sciences liberate, but, even here, the bursting knowledge of the physical sciences is really power to liberate mankind: from hunger, from ignorance and superstition, from grinding poverty and homelessness, all of the conditions that have made millions of persons less than human. But the price of this liberation is value: the value to use the power of science for the humanization rather than the destruction of mankind.

Value is simply central to all that is liberalizing in liberal education. Without value, it would be impossible to visualize liberal education as all that is good in both the intellectual and the moral order of human development and liberation. Along the same line of reasoning, President Robben Fleming of Michigan this year asked his faculty why, in the recent student revolution, it was the liberal arts students who so easily reverted to violence, intolerance, and illiberality. Could it not be that their actions demonstrated that liberal education has begun to fail in the most important of its functions: to liberate man from irrationality, valuelessness, and anomie?

But, one might legitimately ask, how are these great values transmitted in the process of liberal education? All that I have said thus far would indicate that the values are inherent in the teaching of the various disciplines that comprise a liberal education in the traditional sense. However, one should admit that it is quite possible to study all of these branches of knowledge, including those that explicitly treat of values, philosophy and theology, without emerging as a person who is both imbued with and seized by great liberating and humanizing values. I believe that all that this says is that the key and central factor in liberal education is the teacher-educator, his perception of his role, how he teaches, but particularly, how he lives and exemplifies the values inherent in what he teaches. Values are exemplified better than they are taught, which is to say that they are taught better by exemplification than by words.

I have long believed that a Christian university is worthless in our day unless it conveys to all who study within it a deep sense of the dignity of the human person, his nature and high destiny, his opportunities for seeking justice in a very unjust world, his inherent nobility so needing to be realized, for one's self and for others, whatever the obstacles. I would have to admit, even immodestly, that whatever I have said on this subject has had a miniscule impression on the members of our university compared to what I have tried to do to achieve justice in our times. This really says that while value education is difficult, it is practically impossible unless the word is buttressed by the deed.

If all this is true, it means that all those engaged in education today must look to themselves first, to their moral commitments, to their lives, and to their own values, which, for better or worse, will be reflected in the lives and attitudes of those they seek to educate. There is nothing automatic about the liberal education tradition. It can die if not fostered. And if it does die, the values that sustain an individual and a nation are likely to die with it.

In 1966 the late Dr. Rufus Clement, then a colleague of mine on the National Science Board, asked me to address his graduates at that great black educational complex, Atlanta University. I remember the occasion well. I had never addressed an all-black audience before, and, believe it or not, I had never before stayed overnight in a black home. By this time, I had spent almost a decade on the Civil Rights Commission. In fact, we had held a difficult hearing in Atlanta on housing. I decided that civil rights would be my subject at the university.

A word about Rufus Clement. He was one of seven children. Their father was, I believe, a minister. All of the children in this family became professionals: educators, doctors, lawyers, and ministers. I only knew Rufus, who became a dear friend, and I am poorer for not having met the rest of the family. Happily, because of my visit to Atlanta University, I did meet his dear wife, a gracious hostess who made me perfectly at home in their home. I only wish that more white Americans might have had such an experience, not just once, but as casually as we host each other as whites or blacks. Failing this, and the other signs of real friendship, I do not think we will ever solve, at its heart of hearts, the race problem in America.

Years later, I had an update of this experience at Lincoln University below Philadelphia, thanks to another friend, Herman Branson. These are vital institutions. In our newly found zeal to recruit talented black students at prestigious white institutions, we had better not forget that for more than a century, these institutions were their best and only hope. For some black students, they still are.

I write here of the second phase of the civil rights revolution. We have now had more than a decade of this second phase. I must say candidly that it is not going well. The opposition has now gone underground, but it is active. The Supreme Court, which was the hero in the first phase, has recently rendered two decisions which turn back the clock. Its decision on housing in Chicago (Arlington Heights) allows zoning to continue segregated neighborhoods and, obviously, segregated schooling. The recent Indianapolis decision seems to disallow a metropolitan approach to educational integration. As a result, we will be continuing, for the years ahead, bad education in the central city for the blacks and good education in the suburbs for the whites. Has anyone thought what it means for America to have 400,000 poorly educated, in fact uneducated, blacks enter American society each year? This cannot continue unless we really want to create two Americas: one white, prosperous; one black, unemployed and frustrated.

XI

The Civil Rights Revolution: From Confrontation to Education

Most revolutions have two phases. The first phase of the civil rights revolution in America is, I believe, largely over. It accomplished and wrote into federal law the broad lines of what I would call a national conscience on civil rights, a broad national consensus on what every citizen could and should expect of his country and his fellow countrymen in the areas of voting, education, employment, housing, public accommodations, and the administration of justice. Many may still disagree with the consensus, but the national ideal, the law of the land, is clear and is becoming ever more positive.

The second phase of this civil rights revolution is still largely before us, and is more difficult, because it requires the passage from national to individual conscience in recognizing all these rights, and also involves the assumption by all Americans, whatever their color, of the long-range responsibility of living what we profess: to make full, responsible, and intelligent use of these rights, to do in the privacy of each of our lives what we profess in public as Americans. The second phase is largely educational, while the first phase was largely protest. The first phase gave quick results. The second phase will call on all our religious, educational, and social resources to come to full fruition. And it will call for much more courage, patience, perseverance, and understanding. The second phase must move family by family, neighborhood by neighborhood, city by city, state by state to accomplish on the local scene what has been proclaimed on the national scene. This is where each of you comes in, as responsible, educated, individual human beings. This is why each of you is so terribly important. You may or may not have been among the chosen few who moved the first phase of this revolution. The second phase cannot move without each of you. You must become involved or the second phase will fail.

The second striking process of our times is that of human development. The process of human development is the age-old story of man's slow ascent from primitive caverns in the past and from modern slums today, always with the accent on escape from human misery. How many centuries has man's lot been one of ignorance, illness, hunger, alternating cold and heat, minimal shelter, marginal life, and early death? Whatever the estimate, this much is certain, that there has been more effort at human development in our age than in all the ages of man's previous history. Moreover, there are more than twice as many people involved than there were a hundred years ago, and there will be double the present number involved a short forty years hence. There have been more hungry people fed, more sickness cured, more minds educated, more houses built, more clothes manufactured, more books written, more studies made, and more groups formed to promote development in our age than in all the previous ages together.

Not that the problem of human development has been solved; for millions today development is still an aspiration and a hope. But never before has it been possible to even think of a solution on a worldwide basis. Now the process has begun, the concern is born and multiplying, the means are at hand, and something is beginning to happen. What will eventually result is still in question, as the solution to old problems always creates some new problems. The conquest of disease begets a population explosion.

The process of human development is as complicated as the man and the society to be developed. Economic development implies political development, and both presuppose education. Temporal development cannot override man's eternal concerns or man's basic spiritual rights and obligations related to his long-range perfection and maturity as a person. Science cannot substitute for culture, nor the body for the soul in the course of development. The good man and the good society are not simple realities. There can ultimately be no real human development without both of them, and neither can be purchased with money or voted into being or accomplished by technology alone. Again, in the process of human development, we have a movement of significant human change crying for an ultimate meaning and direction that can only come from the involvement of capable, concerned, and dedicated human beings like yourselves.

The third revolutionary instrument of change in our times is the process of technological innovation. Here again, as in the processes of human emancipation and human development, we do not have an absolutely new reality, but a process that is moving so precipitously and on so many different fronts at once that we are hard put to analyze its total impact on our times and ways. You all know the litany of change. Speed increased in a generation from a horse's gallop to a jet traveling through the sound barrier. And then when 3,000 miles an hour had been achieved a few years ago, astronauts suddenly went six times faster. Communication advanced from a few miles' span to millions of miles into space. High energy studies since the war jumped from a few million to many billion electron volts. Astronomy enlarged its field by billions of light years in extent, and by a much wider spectrum of observation through radio telescopes. Biology descended to the molecular level and below. Lasers and semiconductors are again revolutionizing communications and calculations. The developments of one decade in electronic computers reduced problem-solving time from weeks to hours to minutes to billionths of a second. Materials in common use today were unheard of ten years ago. New drugs appear so quickly that even the doctors are often bewildered.

One could go on, but the point should be fairly obvious that technological innovation has created and is creating a vastly different world. Nor is every innovation constructive. No matter how quickly the world's population multiplies, all the earth's people can now be destroyed in a matter of seconds and the earth itself made uninhabitable. The drama of human life has always contained great challenges, but today the drama is bursting through all its traditional limits.

We have spoken only of three revolutionary elements of change. There are many others. All of them are moving, moving ever more quickly, and most of them can best be described as explosive. The least that university graduates can do is to attempt to understand the intellectual content and the meaning of the ideas that lie at the heart of these movements; to plot, insofar as possible in the context of human understanding, where they are and where they should be moving; to see this world as it actually is, not as we would wish it to be by some nostalgic attachment to a more peaceful and stable past, and finally, it would seem imperative that with growing understanding there should also be a growing involvement of university graduates, so that we may somehow guide this change into effective channels.

This will first involve *commitment*. Whatever you value, be committed to it and let nothing distract you from this goal. The uncommitted life, like Plato's unexamined life, is not worth living.

You will also need *compassion*. Compassion means that you suffer with all who suffer, the hungry, the ignorant, the poor, the homeless, the hopeless, the sick, all those who suffer injustice, all who need understanding and help. This is a large order. But you are those privileged few who have been educated, and knowledge is not just knowledge but also power, power to help those who need help.

Of course, you can use your knowledge to help yourself, and only yourself. Many do this, but not the compassionate. In modern parlance, the compassionate get with the revolution to promote human equality, human development, and to use the new science and technology in both of these causes.

Our Lord once said that we must lose our lives to gain them. The compassionate lose themselves in helping others, but in a real sense, they are the only moderns who really learn who they are, what they cherish, what makes their lives rich beyond accounting.

And a necessity is *consecration*. I realize that this is a religious term, but I am sure that you will indulge me thus far. Consecration means that we take gifts we have from God and give them back in service. You know your own gifts better than anyone else. You are free to use them as you will. I cannot tell you that you should use them to make the world better, although I think you should. Whatever I think, you must make the decision, and only you can. I can only say that your gifts are a precious heritage, and that mankind today needs such gifts if human equality, human development, and the promise of science and technology are to become a reality and not a frustrated hope.

Commitment, compassion, and consecration. Three words, these are the sum of my free advice. May you find them sturdy companions.

SECTION FOUR

The Years of Campus Crisis

This section may some day be of historical interest, especially as the troublesome period of the student revolution in the late sixties and early seventies moves further away from us and our memories. Already it seems relatively forgotten, except by those of us who still bear some combat scars and can still recount some very real war stories. For the young freshmen today, it is a period as remote as *Look* and *Life* magazines, which they never saw.

One experience may illuminate the period. I have never written about it before. Just after his first inauguration in 1969, I was visiting alone with President Nixon in the Oval Office of the White House, before tapes were installed. We were discussing civil rights and the poverty program. At the conclusion of the conversation, I decided to be bold. It is not easy in the Oval Office, whoever is president. "Mr. President," I said, "you were just inaugurated, but if the young people I live with could have had their say, 90 percent of them would have voted against your being president, and that is a rather pathological situation that you should do something about." He looked a bit shocked, but was open to suggestions. I offered four: (1) conclude the Vietnam war as soon as possible—it was a major irritant, a red flag to most students; (2) end the draft and institute volunteer armed forces; (3) give eighteen-year-olds the vote; (4) give all American young men and women the opportunity of attending any college or university into which they can be admitted.

Interestingly, under the pressure of the times, President Nixon accomplished all of these four moves, although taking altogether too long getting out of Vietnam. Unfortunately, he had a way of doing it without getting much credit. For my big mouth, I had to spend a year on the Presidential Commission for an All-Volunteer Armed Forces. Anyway, we now have volunteers instead of a draft.

The point of my mentioning this curious corner of history here is that those days, however difficult, did see things done that most probably, without the crisis, would never have happened.

I remember the circumstances of the following chapter all too well in their tragic detail. The day I was to address a commencement audience at the University of Southern California—June 6, 1968—was the day Sen. Robert Kennedy died in Los Angeles from an assassin's bullets. On the way across town, I stopped at the Good Samaritan Hospital to sympathize for a moment with his brother, Sen. Ted Kennedy, and the widows of John and Bob. I told them that I would dedicate my remarks to the memory of these two brothers, with the prayerful hope that their example might be much more persuasive than my words.

XII

In Defense of the Younger Generation

I would like to begin with a quotation from a famous author: "What is happening to our young people? They disrespect their elders, they disobey their parents. They ignore the laws. They riot in the streets inflamed with wild notions. Their morals are decaying. What is to become of them?" These words were written more than twenty-three hundred years ago by Plato, the Greek philosopher.

Another equally famous Greek philosopher, Aristotle, took an almost equally dim view of the young: "Young people have exalted notions, because they have not yet been humbled by life or learned its necessary limitations; moreover, their hopeful disposition makes them think themselves equal to great things. They would always rather do noble deeds than useful ones: their lives are regulated more by moral feelings than by reasoning—all their mistakes are in the direction of doing things excessively and vehemently. They overdo everything—they love too much; hate too much, and the same with everything else."

The generational gap looked much the same twenty-four centuries ago as it has in recent times—to both young and old. I still want to say of the younger generation what Frenchmen are purported to say of women: *vive la différence*—long live the difference between generations. We need it. They do, too.

This is not to say that the difference between generations is always exactly the same—even though Plato and Aristotle may strike a few responsive chords. For one thing, there are not only many more people around today—but also half of them are young people. Twenty years ago, there were 30 million Americans under twenty years of age. Today there are over 80 million Americans under twenty, and, in a few years, half of the population will be aged under twenty-five. This makes the younger generation more visible, more omnipresent, and, let's face it, a very substantial part personally of what America *is*. There is no reason to believe that they will be satisfied to be a silent or passive part of America, either. Nor should they be.

If, as Aristotle says, they love too much and hate too much, that's a whale of a lot of vehement love and hate. But the real question is: What do they love and hate? I suspect that they do not love excessively the world we have created, or at least allow to exist, and I suspect that they hate some things that are well worth hating and difficult to hate excessively: like war, inequality for millions of human beings on earth, poverty in the midst of affluence, hypocrisy in stating one set of values and following another, rhetoric instead of action, promises without fulfillment, empty words—qualities they often find in the adult generation. Maybe the most discouraging thing about youth is that every day they are getting older and on most days the young come of age with the great temptation to become like everyone else, like us, to compromise with the world as it is and ultimately, alas, to become the unwilling target of their own children's ire, as they, the youth of yesteryear, begin to do the useful rather than the noble deeds they once dreamed about in their youth.

Maybe the world of youth is too good to be true and lasting. Maybe instead of being so concerned about the idealism, the generosity, and the vehemence of youth, we should rather mourn the fact that youth passes all too quickly into the grim life of adulthood, when we find it so difficult to really love what is good and hate what is evil, and lose the simplicity of youth that can so easily repeat the prayer of the great Hindu poet, Rabindranath Tagore: "Lord, God, only let me make my life simple and straight, like a flute of reed, for Thee to fill with music.''

In recent years, I have visited many large American cities attempting to raise money for higher education in general and Notre Dame in particular. A dismal task. During the days of student unrest I was asked, "What's happening to this generation? Why the unrest, the protest, the revolt? Why pour so much effort and money into the education of a bunch of kooks?" I admit to a certain amount of unpriestly impatience at this line of questioning. Once, in a New York press conference, I let myself go. "What you're really saying is that unless students are nice fellows like you, we shouldn't be interested in trying to educate them." "I didn't say that," the reporter countered. "Then what are you saying?" I asked. This drew a large silence. I started over again—on the offensive, Notre Dame-like, I confess. "What is so good about you or your world?" I asked this reporter. "Is there nothing to be uneasy about, nothing to protest, nothing to revolt against?" Another silence, with the unspoken question in his eyes: "What set him off?" I tried to explain it. We might begin by trying to understand what caused and still causes the unrest, the protest, the revolt of the young people.

I think there are several immediate causes. First, the young people of today have grown up in an affluent society that prizes intelligence, that provides the best schooling that this country has ever seen. The affluence of many of their parents has freed many of them from the grimy business of worrying where the next dollar is coming from. They have had more time to think, to discuss, to criticize, to read, to travel, to compare, to judge—this is the stuff of which good education is made. And it does have consequences.

In their earlier years, these young people probably took the American dream seriously and uncritically to heart: one nation, indivisible, with liberty and justice for all. How often they recited it in grammar school, without thinking what it really means. Then, for many of them, as they began to think critically, the dream seemed to acquire some of the aspects of a nightmare: they learned that 30 million Americans, Negro, Mexican, Indian, poor white, but mostly black Americans, unlike them, attended inferior schools where twelve years of segregated education equaled only eight or nine years of the white school standard achievement. Partially because of this, much of the best of higher education was foreclosed for these deprived Americans. Then, they found that these 30 million represented twice as many unemployed and unemployable as white, with the young nonwhite, four times as many. Black Americans, they found, generally live in the worst houses, in the worst sections of our cities, and so are fated to continue to attend the worst schools, which are located there, so that their frustration and lack of social mobility upward seem ever circular and inevitable.

Thus, the American nation, they discovered, is not indivisible, but clearly divisible into two nations: black and white, poor and affluent, hopeful and hopeless. Liberty means one thing to the whites, the affluent, and the hopeful, another to the black, the poor, and the hopeless. Justice likewise.

And so this generation of the young began to doubt the sincerity of the slogan they had repeated so often. It was the dawn of disillusionment, a coming of age even in youth. What I say here of the white youngster is, of course, even more poignantly true of the black youngster. For a while, they marched together in the South, together sensed new confidence in the rightness of their cause, new power in what they were able to achieve by protest and organized action against what they knew to be wrong, much less un-American.

Then the blacks, at least many of the new leaders of the new power structure, called black power, decided to go it alone, and the great majority of active, protesting white young people felt momentarily alienated again, with the loss of their newly found cause of civil rights and their active participation in social change.

A new target was quickly found. Escalation gave greater visibility to the war in Vietnam, the draft bit more deeply into the company of the youth, the issues involved were more hotly debated nationally and internationally, and again the young found a new outlet for their newly learned tactics and their yearning for personal involvement in a cause. They aimed indiscriminately at the obvious targets: draft cards, ROTC, Dow and napalm, induction centers, troop trains, and military recruiters. Even the flag took a beating at times, unfortunately, and patriotism, old style, almost became suspect in certain quarters.

Perhaps distracted or possibly annoyed by the noise of it all, too few of the elders really debated the issues or drew back from the mounting cost in lives and dollars. Few really asked about the morality of our national course in spending $30 billion a year tearing up a plot of land and people nowhere near the size and population of the state of California, while the whole wide world of dire human need and misery merited only $2 billion annually in critical assistance, with the bulk of our technical assistance manpower concentrated in the same small plot of land that absorbed over a half-million of our troops at war.

I have somewhat oversimplified and possibly overstated the problem, as do the young, but this was, and is, a real question of justice and morality that has many of our youth hung up as never before. This issue poisoned the atmosphere of our campuses, vitiated many other good and noble endeavors, rocked our national political scene, complicated our foreign relations, and led to a deep and abiding frustration on the part of our youth.

It is one thing to disagree with compulsory military service, or to be disillusioned by the course of a particular war. But the young were angry at the thought of having to take life and face death in a war that they not only did not like, but also often abhorred as alien to all that they think America should be doing in the world.

Some simply copped out, as the saying goes. They became conscientious objectors, or moved to Canada or to the local equivalent of Haight-Asbury, taking refuge in drugs, or bizarre hairdos, or love-ins, or the other appurtenances of hippiedom. It should be said that a very small number took this road, which was, for the few that did, the worst kind of blind alley and dead end. The great majority suffered in quiet frustration or erupted in occasional violence, or worried along, hoping that somehow they would find a personal escape hatch in the walls that seemed to close in around them.

The malaise over Vietnam triggered what I believe to be the

final and probably most important act in the drama of the younger generation: the campus revolt. Having been forced out of meaningful civil rights action, feeling themselves more or less helpless in the face of the Vietnam action which seemed to worsen despite all their protests, the students finally decided that maybe they should seek involvement and reform where they were—in the colleges and universities. After thinking about it for awhile, some even found here the root cause of their alienation from an establishment or a society that they judged to be impersonal, often irrelevant, sometimes immoral, and generally more difficult to move than a cemetery. Again, one must avoid oversimplifications, for the targets for youthful criticism were many: their parents, neighborhoods and cities, their church if they had not already disassociated themselves from it, their adult leadership from the president to their father, anyone exercising authority over them, even those faculty members or deans they judged as really disinterested in them and their lives and, especially, their hopes.

You may ask at this juncture, how did it all get mixed up so quickly, how did the apathetic, uninterested generation of a decade ago suddenly get so critical, so ready to revolt against law and authority in any form, so quick to protest, to sit-in, to lie-in, to tear up-in, to raise hell-in? How did a whole generation get so exercised, so suddenly, about the general state of society and humanity that they began by waving signs in Berkeley and ended by tearing Columbia apart, bringing down the government in Belgium and closing twenty-three of the twenty-seven Italian universities, immobilizing France and the all-powerful de Gaulle, and telling their elders all over the world that everything was going to change or else? However it happened, it did happen and the phenomenon was not local, but national and international. Newspapers in London, Berlin, Tokyo, New York, and Caracas carried similar reporting on the student revolt.

While all of this was explosive, it was not all bad. The world always needs energy, imagination, concern, idealism, dedication, commitment, service. With all its problems, it gets all too little of these great human qualities from the older generation.

The world also needs reasonable criticism and peaceful protest as a constant spur to progress and for the redress of many
horrible inequities and injustices that perdure in the world at
its best. The world needs to change its structures too, because,
obviously, many of them are not producing the climate in
which justice is available to all, not to mention opportunity,
which is even more important to the young.

The problem was that we stimulated the young to hope for
the best. Twenty years ago, for example, the United Nations
proclaimed the Universal Declaration on Human Rights, but it
remained only a declaration, not a fact, for millions of human
beings here and around the world.

We were faced with the challenge of getting the young back
into the human family, as a working part of the establishment,
if you will. The price for this may yet turn out to be a different
kind of establishment, but that may not be a bad idea, either.
Perhaps because I have spent all of my adult life in the world
of the university, it seemed to me that the student revolt
presented an opportunity. After all, we in the universities
stimulated most of the ideas that set off that youthful explosion. We, better than any other part of the total establishment,
should have been able to devise the ways and means of
involving the young in fruitful rather than destructive uses of
their energy and their concern, peaceful rather than violent
outlets for their idealism.

We began by devising new structures in the university for
the active and meaningful participation of the students in
their campus life and education. We did this by trying to
create on campus a real community in which students have a
real and not a phony role. If they were dissatisfied with the
education they were getting, there ought to have been ways
for them to be heard and to have their ideas seriously considered by the faculty and administration. This did not mean
that all their ideas were good or that their desires were always
compelling, and it certainly did not mean that their ideas
should be forced through under threat of violence. Rather,
there arose a dialogue which in itself was educative. One bit of
advice our most active students needed to hear from faculty
was that action is most fruitful when it is backed up, not by

emotion, or mass hysteria, or noise, or violence, but by intelligent and competent leadership, which is the fruit of a good education that is taken seriously during the years when it is available. Students needed to hear that what seemed most relevant to them at that time could be quite irrelevant ten years later. Students needed to hear that action without good ideas and real goals and true values reveals itself eventually as empty posturing, a costly distraction from getting a first-rate education.

Kingman Brewster, then president of Yale University, put it well:

> The tragedy of the highly motivated, impatient young activist is that he runs the serious risk of disqualifying himself from true usefulness by being too impatient to arm himself with the intellectual equipment required for the solution of the problems of war and poverty and indignity. You and I have seen too many among our students of high promise squander their talent for a lifetime of constructive work at a high level, for the cheaper and transient satisfaction of throwing himself on some immediate barricade in the name of involvement. Posturing in the name of a good cause is too often the substitute for thorough thought or the patient doggedness it takes to build something. . . . The chance to make a constructive difference in the lives of others, not the full dinner pail, is the highest reward of a higher education. If the impatient anti-intellectualism of the radical left is not to seduce many of our best brains away from true usefulness, we and our faculties have to reassert again and again that emotional oversimplification of the world's problems is not the path to their solution.

I am in complete agreement with President Brewster, but, in defense of youth, we must see their side, too. They can buy this scheme of things if at least we elders really share their concerns, which should also be our concerns, and do something about them ourselves. We have to face head on and to discuss with students their concern for the relevancy of their education, and how we can improve our university structures to make them a more vital part of the learning community—both inside and outside the classroom. We have to give them an alternative to violent and destructive protest by sharing their concern for meaning in life, and by creating with them right now a meaningful community in the university, with all of us working together to establish and maintain worthwhile goals and values and a vital expression of these in many university activities that are consonant with the university's role as a critic of society and an institution dedicated to the path of wisdom and the achievement of justice for all, not just the favored few.

I am confident that this can be done if the elders have time for the young and if they both can learn to respect each other, and have greater tolerance for each other and for the complementary, rather than competitive, roles that each can play in the university community. Students who like to learn by doing should give their elders credit for having learned something by what they have done, and it is not all bad. The Peace Corps, the Poverty Program, the Teacher Corps, VISTA, new civil rights legislation, the disarmament treaty, tutoring programs in the inner city, the conquest of hunger—all these were devised and launched by the elders, even though most of these programs were given new life and brighter spirit by the young. There can be many more such developments, and they will all make better education and better community life in the university. It is always better to revitalize a basically good system than to destroy it violently while having nothing with which to replace it. And, if that is true of our universities, it is even more true of our families, of our cities, of our nation and our world.

The point is that the young can and should contribute to man's perennial task of remaking the world, especially since they are half of the world that needs remaking. Neither half, young or old, can do it alone. We elders may at times grow restive at their prodding, protest, and revolt, and they may find us impossibly slow when we do not think we can remake anything by tomorrow morning, with or without their help. It is likely that history will repeat itself and the gap between the generations will never be completely bridged by understanding, but I like to believe that there are other workable bridges, at least more workable than anything in common use today, and their names are laughter and love. Indeed, I can think of no better way of redeeming this tragic world today than by love and laughter. Too many of the young have forgotten how to laugh, and too many of the elders have forgotten how to love. Would not the dark tragedy of our life be lightened if only we could all learn to laugh more easily at ourselves and to love one another? It may sound quixotic, but I think this says a lot about the generation gap—how to understand it and how to cure it while we still have time.

This chapter was prepared originally for a 1970 Centennial Symposium at Loyola University in Chicago, two years after the Southern California effort. I am still trying to understand the students, as that was my assignment in the symposium, and I was at the practical task daily, anyway. I try to analyze the world in which they grew of age, a time of cataclysmic and violent change, and the possible effect it had on them. I cite the latest analysis of Margaret Mead on the generation gap and how it operates in times of change. It seemed a valid hypothesis then, but I do not know that it is still valid today. Somehow students seem to have rediscovered their parents, their schools, even their church if it makes some effort to relate to them. I do not think that the young today are presuming to instruct their elders—but they certainly were then.

Unhappily, I do not think that our national priorities have greatly improved either, although I am willing to concede that President Carter is trying mightily to change some of them. Lately, I have been helping launch an international Common Cause–type lobby called "New Directions" that will try to influence some of the current priorities. Margaret Mead, until her death last fall, was helping, too. I find our students anxious to join in this effort.

In 1970, I was concerned with an $80 billion defense budget. Today it is $120 billion and projected for over $150 billion quite soon. While that projection of $30 billion more is taking place, help for the poor of the world to help themselves during the same period is projected for $800 million. The figures change, but the proportions are as bad, if not worse. The figure now for the billion poorest people in some forty nations of the so-called Fourth World is about $150 a year to live on.

While this is happening, the world will spend over $300 billion for arms next year. The World Bank says the true current figure for world armaments is $350 billion, with the developing countries proportionately spending more than the developed countries. The developing countries also spend more on weapons than on health and education. Maybe we need another worldwide youth revolution to protest this idiocy.

XIII

The Generation Gap

So much has been written in recent years about students that, by now, everyone must be tired of the subject, especially the students. They have been described, analyzed, lauded, condemned, advised, threatened, but, perhaps, not very well understood.

One should perhaps begin again on that attempt at understanding—difficult as it is even for those of us who spend our lives with them, difficult, in fact, for students themselves. At least, they realize this as well as, if not better than, the rest of us, since they speak so often of their crisis of identity.

I believe that any attempt at understanding them should begin not with them, but with the world in which they have lived and are living. It is a world of enormous flux and change which must have greatly affected them. There has been more change in their lifetime than in any comparable period in the history of the world. In fact, the past twenty years have seen more change than any thousand years in the past.

What can one say about a generation of young people who have come of age in such a period? If the whole world has been in cataclysmic and violent change during their brief lifetime, can one hope that they would not be influenced by the change and the violence? If all the normal structures were under abnormal stress, what can we say of those whose lives were developing within those trembling and disintegrating

structures? For centuries, young people grew up within com-
paratively stable structures, but this generation has witnessed
the questioning, the challenge, the repudiation of much that
had previously been taken for granted—in the family, the
state, the church, the school. To further complicate the problem, in this country a student population that had grown,
since the beginning of higher education at Harvard in 1636 to 3
million in 1950, grew to 6.5 million during their lifetime, with
all the stresses and instabilities that such rapid growth entails.

I am not sure that anyone really understands the period
through which they and we are passing. Certainly, it is unprecedented in the history of mankind heretofore. It is probably of greater moment than the Renaissance, the Reformation,
the industrial revolution, or the age of exploration. One might
say that so much has been happening, so quickly, that the
human circuits are overcharged and all the normal fuses have
blown out. A large part of the difficulty of understanding the
younger generation today is the very real difficulty of understanding ourselves and the world-in-change in which we all
live. If the older generation has difficulty adjusting to rapid
and unpredictable and unprecedented change, what of the
younger generation, which in the past developed against a
background of relatively unchallenged values of church and
state and family? Given the circumstances, one might wonder
why the situation isn't worse.

Margaret Mead, in a recent book, *Culture and Commitment*,
came up with a threefold classification of relationships between the generations, relating to the rate of social change.
When the rate of change is slow, as it has been for thousands
of years, parents and even grandparents can be models for the
children.

When the rate of social or technological change is so rapid
that the children can no longer be expected to live lives comparable to their parents', parents are no longer models and
their authority is dissipated. Peers become the norms. Here
parents can at least share in their children's advance, and
facilitate it.

In the third state, our present situation, change is so rapid
that parents can neither prepare their children for emancipa-

tion nor accept it. Communication between the generations is reversed; parents can and must learn from their children, who are more at home in the present world than the parents are. This is at best a most difficult and, up to now, unheard of situation, requiring good will and understanding almost beyond comprehension. This is the measure of our present situation.

When one looks sympathetically at the younger generation today, several trends are clearly discernible. At the outset, one should admit that students, like every other group, are not a single reality—there are the far-out, the great central group, and the conservatives. What I say, then, can only be taken as a generality, not applicable to all.

First, the younger generation share the questioning applicable to the age in which we live. They question the values long assumed to be true and absolute, like patriotism linked solely to the military; industrial enterprise as free, liberal, and always on the side of the angels; democracy within which minorities have never had equal liberty and justice; higher education in which research has often outshone teaching; society and bigness of organization leading to impersonalization and alienation; families characterized more by status seeking and social ambition than by human sensitivity and love. In this questioning, the young have become the conscience of the status quo—a shattering experience for the older generation, who have traditionally been the mentors of the young. The rebellion has been heightened by the imaginative rebellion of the young against the standards of the elders—long hair and sloppy dress; incivility in speech and attitude; feeling substituted for rationality and dramatized by a drug usage to heighten feeling; bohemianism to shock the elders in the complete repudiation of all they hold sacred and standard.

It has been said that only an affluent culture could provide youth with the means to mount such an offensive against the accepted values of a society. Their parents did not have the financial means to do other than conform and work within the system to survive. This generation enjoys repudiating the system that sustains them.

Are they ingrates? Should they be put to the hard test of work and puritanical values that bred their elders? Should they be roundly condemned for contaminating their nest?

I think not. Possibly they are our salvation in these troubling times, when we of the older generation may have too much of the baggage of the past to make the clear-cut decisions that are too easy for the young, who bring to our present situation a freshness of the dawn and unencumbered judgment, a new insight. In saying this, I am not succumbing to the current cult of juvenocracy that says that the young can do no wrong and that they should be followed wherever they lead. They do have insights, idealism, and generosity of spirit—as the young always have had—but they have their faults, too—mainly, naiveté, lack of experience and contempt for it, simplistic solutions for very complicated problems, impatience with the time that meaningful change requires.

What I am really proposing is that there is much to be learned and much to be resisted in the thrust that comes to us from the students of today. They are at times very perceptive and at times very stupid; they have insight and blindness; their idealism is faulted by their inherent lack of discipline, and they are, like all young people of all times, more given to the activism of the moment than to the contemplation and wisdom that make action meaningful.

We cannot really fault them for this, for it is a fault that we all shared at their age, maybe not to the extent that they now manifest it, but they grew up in quite a different age than we did. What I am really seeking is understanding that will somehow take into account all that is valid in what they are saying, with all the other validities that we can bring to their message.

To do this will not be easy, for the older generation has always been impatient and demanding of the younger. Yet, today we are all together seized by the extraordinary exigencies of our times, and we need all the wisdom we can bring to bear upon our problems, be it youthful insight or older knowledge.

Perhaps we might begin by recognizing certain givens—such as human dignity and liberty, the open society, the quality of life characterized by a few fixed values, such as honesty, love, a desire for peace or nonviolence, competence as opposed to dilettantism, rationality as opposed to blind feeling, spirituality as opposed to materialism, civility as opposed to incivility and vulgarity, respect as opposed to contempt for persons.

If we, young and old, can agree on these basic values that make human life worth living, then perhaps we can pool our efforts, young and old, to redeem the times. It still won't be easy, but it can be done.

What it means is that each of us, young and old, will have to listen more to each other, to respect each other more than we have heretofore. We will have to learn from each other, to work more in concert to create a better world.

The elders who have thus far compromised to live with violence will now have to question it as the young do. The young who are so enthusiastically given to their often simplistic point of view will have to be more open to differing points of view.

Above all, we will have to reconsider together the priorities of our national life today: the deep and complicated questions of war and peace; equality of opportunity for all our people and the people of the Third and Fourth Worlds; the state of our cities and the pollution of our total environment; the quality of American life, which is so much a function of the quality of American education on all levels; the actual status of the military-industrial complex, which is a tiger at our gates to be controlled rather than endured.

It is my solemn judgment that we can undertake this enterprise together, young and old, and do it better together—each counterbalancing the other—rather than by confronting each other by extreme approaches. This is not a world of the young or the old, but our world which we share together, and we need every possible insight if we are to make it humanly habitable.

The older generation today infuriates the younger by projecting this as a world of law and order. I believe we might achieve the best of all worlds by proclaiming to the young that we do not conceive law and order as ends in themselves, but as a matrix, an environment within which we can best achieve justice and equality of opportunity for all our citizens.

This stance means fundamentally that we do not accept law and order as status quo—things as they are. One could only do this if ours were a perfect world—which it is not.

What do the students of today find wrong in our world? Mostly priorities—as revealed in our national budget. We say that peace is important—while we spend about half our budget for war. We continue to make encouraging pledges— such as a recent one to build 28 million new houses in a decade—while continuing to spend 100 times more for defense than housing, despite the fact that millions of our citizens live in condemned and dilapidated housing. We are willing to spend additional billions for an ABM system, while cutting money from education in the name of avoiding inflation. Four presidents in a row have told me that civil rights are our most pressing domestic problem. Yet at one time the budget of the United States Commission on Civil Rights was frozen at $2,650,000, one-third of the cost of a military fighter aircraft that survived about one week in a war such as Vietnam.

By percentage of per capita income, or GNP, we are seventh in the world of nations in what we spend to develop mankind, one-half of which must subsist on a family income of $100 a year.

The students ask: Are we really concerned, compassionate, ready to help create a new world, at home and abroad? Here at home we are creating, not what all of them recited in grade school each morning, "one nation, indivisible, with liberty and justice for all"—but two nations: one black or brown, and one white; one educated, one uneducated; one poor, one affluent; one with hope, the other hopeless.

Only recently have we become as concerned abroad with human development as we have been with military alliances.

Thank God, they are concerned—we are all too little concerned. They believe in the virtue of compassion for mankind, so often the victim of man's inhumanity to man. They sense that law and order are not possible in a world, or in a nation, or in a university in which there is not a deep concern for justice and equality and the development of a better world.

Granting all their impatience and naiveté in the face of tremendously complicated problems, may we at least hope that they will avoid the curse, the vice, the cancer that afflicts so much of modern society—the condition we characterize as *anomie*.

Anomie means restlessness, a spiritual vacuum, a lack of values, a drifting, a complete lack of conviction regarding what is important for our times in the way of priorities, values, or the ultimate meaning of life, individual or societal.

Anomie is all around us today, but generally it has not afflicted them, thank God. Just this week one of our students asked me a very difficult question: "How do you know God, how do you perceive him, contact him, relate to him?"

I told him that God, for me, was Christ Incarnate, fully God, fully man, joining in his person God and man, the hopes, the desires, hungers of man with the transcendence of God. And when Christ left us, he promised us the Holy Spirit to abide with us, to guide us, to give us what we find as the recurring theme of Saint John's Gospel: life and light—light to guide us and life to live divinely.

Nothing less is needed to find our way out of the labyrinth of human problems today—with the light of divine guidance. No anomie here. Rather a sense of compassion, joined to the hope of a better tomorrow—whatever it may bring in the nature of new challenges, new insights, new demands of divinely inspired human courage. This is the good import of modern student concerns.

We are moving with the rapidity of a new age aborning, almost too fast for any of us to comprehend. But I do believe that together, young and old, communicating and understanding, we can bring to this new age the wisdom ever new and ever old that characterizes the church and the Christian message and, hopefully, the Christian university.

Anything less than generosity, idealism, and dedication of our total being will not do. Anything less than the wisdom of the ages, joined to the insight of the new age, will not suffice. We need both and both are available. The only real problem is to bring them to bear together on our problems. This, I think, can be done if we only will do it—with understanding and forbearance, compassion and great good will on behalf of both the young and the older generation. It was for this task that universities and colleges came to be. May this be their continuing and most important task in the days ahead.

When I addressed the American Council on Education, keynoting their annual fall meeting in Washington in 1971, everyone hoped that the campus crisis was over and that now we might objectively assess the wreckage. There was a measure of peace in the land. We had another crisis ahead, but that would be governmental, not educational, except that we had to learn from Watergate, too.

In this chapter, directed to the leaders of American education, most of them newly appointed, I try to show what happened to the basic elements of our system, to community, to moral leadership and moral consensus, to concern for the well-being of the whole enterprise of higher education. I take a look at the climate, which sadly called for a reestablishment of credibility and trust, something we had always taken for granted. The basic question to be asked of a fairly shaken assembly is: "Where do we go from here, knowing what we now know, accepting responsibility for where we failed, moving forward again with renewed hope?" The wild academic growth problem would take care of itself in the years ahead. Our hopes would now be more realistic, since we had learned that we could not solve every problem under the sun, not even some affecting ourselves and our institutions. More intellectual and moral leadership would be needed. We also needed more personal responsibility up and down the academic ladder, from trustees, presidents, faculty, students, and alumni, too. This was obviously a time for rebuilding.

It was a sober time, but I think that we have reestablished our credibility, indicating that we did learn the lessons that emerged from the worst crisis that afflicted American higher education in its more than three centuries of existence. Fortunately, it was also the shortest, lasting only about five years. It seemed longer, but then we were in the middle of it.

XIV

The Lessons of the
Student Revolution

During the days of campus unrest, it was difficult to be standing there when the dam gave way and not get wet. I recall one brief period when one president was unhorsed because he called in the police, and another fell because he did not. I asked one great president how he had survived a difficult crisis and he answered with great humility: "Each morning when I dragged myself from bed, I asked myself, 'What is the worst thing I could do today?' and I didn't do it."

However one explains the worldwide revolution in higher education, in the case of the revolution in American higher education all the usual problems were exacerbated by the Vietnam war, racial conflict, sudden realization of the plight of the poor in the midst of plenty, wastage and pillage of our national resources, the horrible state of national priorities as reflected in the federal budget, and, in general, by the increasingly dismal quality of our national life. Having made little progress in their assault on racial injustice and the inanity of the Vietnam war, the young—an unprecedented proportion of whom were now college and university students for a variety of right and wrong reasons—turned their frustrations on the institution closest to hand, their college or university. The other problems continued to grind away, so that the new revolution fed upon itself as frustration here was heightened by impatience there, and impatience there by frustration here.

There was enough wrong within the colleges and universities, too, so that we soon had an ever more explosive mixture awaiting simple ignition. There were plenty of volunteers to light the match. Every succeeding explosion on one campus ignited others elsewhere. And so it went across the country from West to East and back again. Few institutions escaped unscarred, some were profoundly changed, and all were affected in one way or another. Some looked in the face of death, and that more than anything else may have accounted for the detente.

What really was wrong within the colleges and universities that fueled the fires of revolution? Strangely enough, we were the victims of our own success. Higher education in its earlier American version grew slowly, from the founding of Harvard in 1636 to a national total of 50,000 college students in 1900. For the last century, this student body doubled every fifteen years. This was hardly a herculean task when the doubling meant going from 12,500 to 25,000 students, or from 25,000 to 50,000, or even from 50,000 to 100,000.

But by the early 1950s, we had a base of 3 million which in doubling to 6 million and then moving towards 12 million meant doing educationally in 15 years more than had been done in the last 330 years. We were all so busy growing and expanding, reaching towards the enrollment of half the age group in higher education, that we did not have time to ask whether what was good for 50,000, or 2 percent of the college age group in 1900, was equally good for 8½ million, or 40 percent of the college age group in 1970.

Moreover, change during all these decades has meant simply and mostly expansion and growth externally but not necessarily internally, more of the same for ever greater numbers of students, more of the same kind of faculty teaching the same kinds of courses. This may make sense in the production of more hot dogs, but growth in higher education certainly must mean more than simple reduplication of what is and has been.

Suddenly the students asked the question we had all been too busy to ask—does this whole enterprise, as presently constituted, really provide a good education for everyone? I grant that their suggestions for internal change were not always an obvious move towards certain educational improvement, but they did start us looking more seriously at what we were doing, and it is no secret that we were not always greatly pleased by what we saw within our institutions.

Some of our most distinguished and most highly compensated faculty were teaching less and less and seeing students only when unavoidable, while graduate students carried on the bulk of teaching for slave wages. New faculty, by the tens of thousands, were trained annually for research, engaged to teach, and most rewarded when they could negotiate lucrative contracts from government, industry, or foundations that took them away from both campus teaching and on-campus, course-related research that involved their students as well as themselves and their careers. Four distinguished Midwestern universities once boasted that almost 400 of their faculty were presently overseas, and the standard joke was the Pan-American Faculty Chair that took the distinguished holder somewhere, anywhere but to the university.

Administrators were getting their share of the bounty too: not only balancing their budgets with the ever-enlarging research contract overhead funds, but also traveling about to see how the overseas or off-campus enterprises were coming along, and finding additional time to lend their distinguished presence to all manner of industrial, governmental, military, or other activities. Meanwhile, at home, liberal education, the core of the whole endeavor, became fragmented, fractured, and debilitated, as subspecialty was heaped on subspecialty, and students learned more and more about less and less, and next to nothing about the great humanistic questions, such as the meaning of life and death, war and peace, justice and injustice, love and hatred, art and culture, to mention a few.

Few educators even adverted to the fact that this enormous growth in their student bodies did not include those who needed higher education most—minority youngsters and children of the lower socioeconomic quartile of the population, for whom a college degree was the essential ingredient to upward mobility and who, whatever their talent or native intelligence, had only one-seventh of the chance to enter higher education as did the youngsters from the upper socioeconomic quartile, whatever their intelligence or promise.

The total structure of higher education remained largely the same, although the enterprise doubled every fifteen years and quadrupled every thirty years. Student questioning about governance caught most colleges and universities flat-footed. In their eagerness to reform, many institutions overcompensated, so that, from being badly governed, they now emerged as largely ungovernable. Every decision now has to run the gauntlet of many potential vetoes from every conceivable quarter within and outside the university. This, too, compounded the internal problems, since a wise man with some plausible solutions to assist the ailing institution could die of old age before seeing them realized.

My account of internal problems is far from complete, but before leaving this first point—why the revolution of the past few years?—may I add one more potent factor of failure. Most colleges and universities during, and possibly because of, their rapid growth simply ceased to be communities. Almost everyone was culpable. Trustees were often simply unrepresentative of the total endeavor they ultimately sought to govern. One distinguished Western university had a board of trustees that was consistently wealthy, male, white, aged, Western, Republican, and Protestant. Read backwards, this means that there were generally no middle or lower class trustees, no blacks or Chicanos or Orientals, no women or younger people, no Catholics or Jews, no Middle-Western, Southern, or Eastern members, and, generally, no Democrats. One might ask how such trustees can provide wisdom for a community that contained reasonably large numbers of all the elements not represented on the board.

One might wonder why presidents and top administrators in higher education did not see the storm coming and strengthen their communities to meet it effectively. An obvious answer would be that the storm burst suddenly and that the community had been already badly eroded. Rather than strengthened, the community had to be recreated and this was no easy task when part of the crisis was a lack of community, or an external quasi-community that lacked credibility, legitimacy, or even the will to govern itself.

If one must fault presidents and chancellors among others, and we must, it would have to be for a lack of moral leadership, not just in time of crisis, but more consistently in earlier and peaceful times. We too often were blind to the moral implications of unbridled educational growth that was certainly spectacular but questionably educational. We did not use our influence to move for more representative boards of trustees, greater rewards for those faculty concerned with students, teaching, and true educational reform and growth, more minority students, and stronger words at times for those students who clamored for responsible freedom without being responsible once granted greater freedom. We might also have labored more aggressively in the continuing education of our alumni, who have their own new problems understanding each new age and change.

Once we washed our hands of any moral concern for all that was happening in our academic communities, we reaped the harvest of a disintegrating community. I grant that the great wisdom and courage required for moral leadership are not common qualities among men and women, but then neither are college or university presidencies common tasks. I grant as well that, in its early stages, disintegration of a community is almost imperceptible to all but the very wisest and that, as disintegration brings on a crisis of legitimacy and credibility, superhuman courage and charisma are needed to recreate what has been largely lost.

In any case, most presidents paid their individual price for a situation created by many, not least of all by the wild men among the student body, most of whom have now successfully graduated, and by some irresponsible faculty members who are still around now that the scapegoat has been driven into the desert. No need to lament further, only to learn from all that happened. There is an interesting Gospel story of the man from whom a devil was driven, only to be later repossessed by seven worse devils.

What then can we learn from all that has happened? First, I think, that moral leadership is as vitally important to a community as the participation of all its members in its healthy life and growth. Participation has been the word most popularly voiced following the crisis, but there has been all too little said about the moral imperatives of this participation. I have a strong belief, nurtured no doubt by my own prejudices, that the central person in exercising moral leadership for the life and prosperity of any academic institution must be its president. He must, first and foremost, speak for the priorities that really count in academia. Presidential leadership demands that, for his speaking to be effective, he must somehow enlist the support of the various segments of the community. Otherwise, he is only speaking for himself and to himself, which is good posturing, but bad leadership.

There is no magic formula for presidential leadership. Each president must establish his own credibility. He will do this best by the goals which shine through his own life and activities. The day of Olympian detachment for presidents is over. If justice needs a voice, on campus or off, he must have the wisdom and courage to say what must be said, and the president must not be the last one to say it. If faculty or students need defense, he should be the first to defend them. If either or both need criticism, the president cannot avoid saying honestly and clearly what is wrong. If the learning process is lagging because of glacial progress in reforming curricula, structures, teaching, and inflexible, outmoded requirements, the president must remind the community of what is needed for educational growth and survival in an unprecedented changing world. He must blow the trumpet loudly and clearly, because the times demand it. There was a time when a president was expected to be a lion abroad and a mouse at home. No longer.

The president, above all other members in the community, must portray respect for the mind and its special values, for true learning and culture, for humanity and humane concerns, for academic freedom, for justice and equality, in all that the university or college touches, especially the lives of its students, faculty, and alumni. Of course, the name of the game is good communications on every level, at every opportunity, but I must insist that the president communicates best by what he is and what he does with his own life. If he has credibility, then the goals he proposes will be the extension of that credibility and the means of welding the community together.

While the community is primarily academic, I submit once more that its basis of unity must be of the heart as well as of the head. It was not merely intellectual problems that recently unraveled great institutions of learning across the world, but rather the dissipation of moral consensus, community, and concern. When members of a college or university stop caring about each other or their institution, or become unclear about personal or institutional goals, then community ceases to be and chaos results.

The mystique of leadership, be it educational, political, religious, commercial, or whatever, is next to impossible to describe, but wherever it exists, morale flourishes, people pull together towards common goals, spirits soar, order is maintained, not as an end in itself, but as a means to move forward together. Such leadership always has a moral as well as an intellectual dimension; it requires courage as well as wisdom; it does not simply know, it also cares. When a faculty and a student body know that their president really cares about them, they will follow him to the heights, even out of the depths.

Moreover, good leadership at the top inspires correlative leadership all down the line. Participatory democracy cannot simply mean endless discussion. Rather, if it is to work at all, it means that every member of the community, especially within his or her own segment of the community, exercises moral responsibility, especially when it hurts and when it demands the courage to say and do what may be unpopular. Student judicial courts will not survive if they never find anyone guilty or never impose adequate sanctions for obvious wrongdoing. Student government will soon enough lose all credibility and acceptance, even from students, if its only concerns are freer sex, more parking, education without effort, and attainment of the heights of utopia without climbing. Faculty senates will only be debating societies if they never recognize the central faculty abuses and move effectively to correct them. Vice-presidents and deans and departmental chairmen do not exist to pass the buck upwards and to avoid the difficult decisions. Leadership may be most important at the presidential level, but it is absolutely essential at every level—trustees, faculty, administrators, students, and alumni—if the community is going to be equal to the task that lies ahead for each college and university and for the total enterprise of higher education in America.

This brings me to my final point: Where do we go from here? First, I think we should clearly understand the climate that results from the events of the past years in academia. For the first time in more than a century, the end of quantitative growth in higher education is in sight. Having doubled in size every fifteen years during the last century, we now see higher education leveling off by 1980, possibly slipping downward a bit. This latter movement is already perceptible in graduate education.

However, there is a more serious aspect to the climate in which we in higher education now live. After a century when the society at large could not do enough for universities and colleges, when these institutions represented the epitome of just about everyone's hopes, a degree being the closest earthly replica of the badge of salvation, suddenly the great American public, our patron and faithful supporter, is rather completely disillusioned about the whole enterprise, let down, as they say, by the weak, vacillating, spineless presidents, their former darlings, disgusted by the ultraliberal, permissive faculties who were going to solve all of the world's problems but could not solve their own, and, needless to say, revolted by the students in more ways than one, despite the fact that these are their own sons and daughters, the products of the most primordial education of all, which does, or does not, take place in the family.

It is paradoxical that at a time when the universities are being asked to solve more problems than ever before—urban blight, racial tensions, minority opportunity, generation gap, overseas development, environmental pollution, political participation by the young, forward motion in atomic energy and space, and a whole host of other concerns—at this same time we are misunderstood, abused, and abandoned as never before by government and foundations, by benefactors, parents, and alumni, and generally by the public at large.

From what I have said already, it is obvious that we are not blameless at this moment in time. I will not repeat our faults. Most dramatically, in the eyes of the public, our institutions, which were supposed to have answers for everyone and everything, had few answers for ourselves and our own troubles; the citadels of reason fell to the assaults of mindless emotion; the centers of taste and civility spouted obscenities; the havens of halcyon peace and pranks saw within them violence, destruction, and even death.

We must admit that we were given magnificent coverage in the media when we were at our worst, and although the worst, in terms of delinquent persons and horrible events, represented a very small corner of the total scene, the stereotypes came through clearly and tended to be universalized. The centuries-old love affair of American society with higher education suddenly turned to ashes. And now, at our time of greatest opportunity and direst financial crisis, we are spurned by the very people who created us, confided their children to us, supported us, and looked to us for a solution to everything difficult.

Perhaps one central problem is that we encouraged and allowed the public to place too much hope in us, to expect too much of our endeavor, to be too confident of our apparent omnipotence when, in fact, there are simply many important tasks that we cannot do without perverting what we were established to do. We are not the state or the church, the Red Cross or the Peace Corps, not the Overseas Development Council or the Legal Aid Society. Our members may be active in any or all of these bodies, but we are not these bodies and we cannot institutionally do their work. No wonder that hopes were frustrated when we suggested or allowed hope to transcend the reality of what we are and what we really should be doing.

Not only our supporters in government and the private sector, but also our students expected from us something far beyond higher education and, of course, received less.

A Harvard professor, Richard Pipes, has stated it well: "The dissolution of family and community life and the decline of secondary education have produced a generation of college students, many of whom no longer seek at the university learning and social pleasures, but also and above all affection, attention, moral guidance, and an opportunity to become personally involved in adult affairs. The universities are not equipped to provide these things."

Personally, I believe we have come out of the crisis more disposed to provide for our students affection, attention, moral guidance, and an opportunity to become personally involved in adult affairs. The vote for eighteen-year-olds looms more important than military service. We have been listening harder to our students, which spells attention. We have learned that it is difficult to educate those we do not really love, and I trust I have already said enough about the moral dimension of higher education.

Perhaps during the period of rapid growth, we grew beyond our potential to be personal and human. High on the list of our agenda now must be how to correct this. As mentioned above, the faculty, the heart of the whole endeavor, were often seduced by the possibility of being rewarded more and more for teaching less and less. Tenure too often became a safe opportunity for somnolence rather than a call to be different, to dare, and to excel. Trustees and presidents were too often too busy with the wrong things. Students were generally on target, but not always on the right one, especially when autocriticism was required. We were all less than we could and should have been. We were all caught up in unusual historical currents in a very troubled, unjust, and unpeaceful world, yes, but we still must answer for ourselves and our personal responsibility to remake our own world of higher education in a better image.

Anyway, I began with the hope that the worst may be over. Ours is a resilient enterprise—see how it grew—and we may well be better for the many tragedies we have experienced during the past five years. Clark Kerr recently said that American higher education has entered its second climacteric in more than a third of a millennium of its existence. That may be fearsome, but it is also exciting. According to Kerr, the last climacteric lasted fifty years, roughly from 1820 to 1870. Those 50 years were difficult; they saw many changes, but they were the prelude to the century of extraordinary growth that we have just experienced. May our second climacteric also be the prelude to better days ahead.

There is little profit in just licking our wounds or feeling sorry for ourselves. We still represent the best hope for America's future, provided that we learn from our own mistakes and reestablish in the days ahead that which so often testified to the nobility of our endeavors in times past. All is not lost. We are simply beginning again, as man always must, in a world filled with ambiguities, the greatest of which is man himself.

XV

A Case Study: Universities and Government Interact in Crisis

There came a time in the crisis when everything seemed to go out of control—here, there, and everywhere. I had a hunch that it was time to blow the whistle or we were all in very serious trouble, with the irate public, with the National Guard, with the local police. The hard hats were spoiling for a fight, anyway. It seemed to me that the time had come to draw a line, to spell out the conditions governing protest very clearly, to enunciate the controlling principles, and then to say, this is it. So far, and no further. No one had really done this. Some, I think, were afraid to draw the line because they really did not know if they could enforce it, or if they would be backed by their faculty, students, and alumni. The total community was both shaky and uncertain.

We had a few crises at Notre Dame, each one more difficult than the one before, which meant to me, at least, that there was more to come and it would be worse.

I decided to do two things: first, to draw the lines as best I could, taking neither a total hawkish nor a total dovish approach, but appealing to the best in both camps. Second, I put everyone's feet to the fire and asked them to declare openly, and for publication, whether they would back this approach or not. It took some arm twisting, but finally all of the constituent bodies of faculty, colleges, students, and alumni said they would back my stand, each on their own terms and with their own misgivings. The only college missing from our five was Arts and Letters (we have a distinct College of Science). But I did have the backing of the Academic Council (our highest academic body) and the Faculty Senate. We were between meetings of trustees, but I knew they would back me.

At this juncture, I announced the policy in a letter sent to every student and faculty member, every administrator and trustee. Somehow it touched a live nerve. Within two days it was in every paper in the country and carried in full in the *New York Times*. Unfortunately, as so often happens, the press overemphasized the tough part in the middle of the letter and hardly mentioned the beginning and end, which spoke of the legitimacy of protest, for proper reasons and with proper means. I came off sounding like a superhawk. Then began a new crisis.

I was on my way to an annual meeting of the Conference on Higher Education in the American Republics, held that year in Bogotá, Colombia. En route, I stopped over for a day in Miami with one of our trustees. He had a horse racing at Hialeah that day and asked me to accompany him to the track. I had never been to an American horse race before. When we returned to the hotel, all the staff people said at once, "The president has been calling you. We had to tell him where you were." A four-page telegram then arrived from President Nixon congratulating me on my stand. He added that while he was leaving immediately for Europe, Vice-President Agnew would be having a meeting of all the state governors in a few days and I should advise him regarding federal legislation regulating turmoil on the campuses of the country, since the vice-president would be discussing the subject with the governors.

At this point, my heart sank. Repressive legislation was the last thing we wanted or needed. I certainly did not want anything to do with it, and had to head it off in any way possible. But I was leaving for Bogotá in a few hours.

Once in Bogotá, I took the first free moments to frame a suitable cable to the vice-president. Fortunately, two old and very capable friends agreed to read and criticize my initial draft, Sol Linowitz, then the American ambassador to the

Organization of American States, and Alex Heard, chancellor of Vanderbilt. They were both very helpful. Once the final draft was ready, I asked the American ambassador to Colombia to send it. He said he was having trouble with communications, but would try. (It never arrived.) Then, being worried, I tried a different route. That did not work either, although I did not know it at the time. But my instincts were working overtime. The morning that the meeting of the governors was to begin, I met Sol Linowitz and his wife, Toni, checking out in the lobby of the Tequendama. I told Sol about my worry that the cable would not arrive on time. He promised to go directly from the Washington airport to the White House and deliver it by hand to Pat Moynihan, who would quickly sense its importance. He did so. Pat had fifty copies made immediately and took them to the governors' meeting, right away.

Gov. Nelson Rockefeller later told me that it was a real cliffhanger. The discussion was going badly from our point of view. More than forty governors were ready to vote for repressive legislation against the universities. Then Pat Moynihan arrived with the cable. They took time to read it and suddenly the vote turned completely around, with more than forty against repressive legislation. Moral of the story: follow your instincts and thank God you have friends like Sol and Pat.

At that time, I think a lot of people liked me for the wrong reasons, but the crisis did quiet down temporarily and take a turn for the better. Resistance to violence, incivility, and boorishness began to stiffen. Also, the experience may explain why I spent so much time after 1969 trying to get people to understand why the students were legitimately upset and what was good about their concerns. A hawk I am not.

Now that the story is told, some may like to read the original letter to the students that triggered all this, as well as the cable to Vice-President Agnew that almost did not get delivered on time.

February 17, 1969

Dear Notre Dame Faculty and Students:

This letter has been on my mind for weeks. It is both time and overtime that it be written. I have outlined the core of it to the Student Life Council, have discussed the text with the chairman of the Board of Trustees, the Vice-Presidents' Council, all the deans of the university, and the chairmen of the Faculty Senate and the Student Life Council. This letter does not relate directly to what happened here last weekend, although those events made it seem even more necessary to get this letter written. I have tried to write calmly, in the wee hours of the morning when at last there is quiet and pause for reflection.

My hope is that these ideas will have deep personal resonances in our own community, although the central problem they address exists everywhere in the university world today and, by instant communication, feeds upon itself. It is not enough to label it the alienation of youth from our society. God knows there is enough and more than enough in our often nonglorious civilization to be alienated from, be you young, middle-aged, or old.

The central problem to me is what we do about it and in what manner, if we are interested in healing rather than destroying our world. Youth especially has much to offer—idealism, generosity, dedication, and service. The last thing a shaken society needs is more shaking. The last thing a noisy, turbulent, and disintegrating community needs is more noise, turbulence, and disintegration. Understanding and analysis of social ills cannot be conducted in a boiler factory. Compassion has a quiet way of service. Complicated social mechanisms, out-of-joint, are not adjusted with sledgehammers.

The university cannot cure all our ills today, but it can make a valiant beginning by bringing all its intellectual and moral powers to bear upon them: all the idealism and generosity of its young people, all the wisdom and intelligence of its oldsters, all the expertise and competence of those who are in their middle years. But it must do all this as a university does, within its proper style and capability, no longer an ivory tower, but not the Red Cross either.

Now to the heart of my message. You recall my letter of November 25, 1968. It was written after an incident, or happening, if you will. It seemed best to me at the time not to waste time in personal recriminations or heavy-handed discipline, but to profit from the occasion to invite this whole university community, especially its central councils of faculty, administration, and students, to declare themselves and to state their convictions regarding protests that were peaceful and those that threatened the life of the community by disrupting the normal operations of the university and infringing upon the rights of others.

I now have statements from the Academic Council, the Faculty Senate, the Student Life Council, some college councils, the Alumni Board, and a whole spate of letters from individual faculty members and a few students. Some of these are enclosed in this letter. In general, the reaction was practically unanimous that this community recognizes the validity of protest in our day—sometimes even the necessity—regarding the current burning issues of our society: war and peace, especially Vietnam; civil rights, especially of minority groups; the stance of the university vis-à-vis moral issues of great public concern; the operation of the university as university. There was also practical unanimity that the university could not continue to exist as an open society dedicated to the discussion of all issues of importance if protests were of such a nature that the normal operations of the university were in any way impeded, or if the rights of any member of this community were abrogated, peacefully or nonpeacefully. I believe that I now have a clear mandate from this university community to see that: (1) our lines of communication between all segments of the community are kept as open as possible, with all legitimate means of communicating dissent assured, expanded, and protected; (2) civility and rationality are maintained as the most reasonable means of dissent within the academic community; and (3) violation of others' rights or obstruction of the life of the university are outlawed as illegitimate means of dissent in this kind of open society. Violence was especially deplored as a violation of everything that the university community stands for.

Now comes my duty of stating, clearly and unequivocally, what happens if. I'll try to make it as simple as possible to avoid misunderstanding by anyone. May I begin by saying that all of this is hypothetical and I personally hope it never happens here at Notre Dame. But, if it does, anyone or any group that substitutes force for rational persuasion, be it violent or nonviolent, will be given fifteen minutes of meditation to cease and desist. They will be told that they are, by their actions, going counter to the overwhelming conviction of this community as to what is proper here. If they do not within that time period cease and desist, they will be asked for their identity cards. Those who produce these will be suspended from this community as not understanding what this community is. Those who do not have or will not produce identity cards will be assumed not to be members of the community and will be charged with trespassing and disturbing the peace on private property and treated accordingly by the law. The judgment regarding the impeding of normal university operations or the violation of the rights of other members of the community will be made by the Dean of Students. Recourse for certification of this fact for students so accused is to the tripartite Disciplinary Board established by the Student Life Council. Faculty members have recourse to the procedures outlined in the Faculty Manual. Judgment of the matter will be delivered within five days following the facts, for justice deferred is justice denied to all concerned.

After notification of suspension, or trespass in the case of non-community members, if there is not then within five minutes a movement to cease and desist, students will be notified of expulsion from this community and the law will deal with them as nonstudents.

Lest there by any possible misunderstanding, it should be noted that law enforcement in this procedure is not directed at students. They receive academic sanctions in the second instance of recalcitrance and, only after three clear opportunities to remain in student status, if they still insist on resisting the will of the community, are they then expelled and become nonstudents to be treated as other nonstudents, or outsiders.

There seems to be a current myth that university members are not responsible to the law, and that somehow the law is the enemy, particularly those whom society has constituted to uphold and enforce the law. I would like to insist here that all of us are responsible to the duly constituted laws of the university community and to all of the laws of the land. There is no other guarantee of civilization versus the jungle or mob rule, here or elsewhere.

If someone invades your home, do you dialogue with him or call the law? Without the law, the university is a sitting duck for any small group from outside or inside that wishes to destroy it, to incapacitate it, to terrorize it at whim. The argument goes—or has gone—invoke the law and you lose the university community. My only response is that without the law you may well lose the university—and beyond that—the larger society that supports it and that is most deeply wounded when law is no longer respected, bringing an end to everyone's most cherished rights.

I have studied at some length the new politics of confrontation. The rhythm is simple: (1) find a cause, any cause, silly or not; (2) in the name of the cause, get a few determined people to abuse the rights and privileges of the community so as to force a confrontation at any cost of boorishness or incivility; (3) once this has occurred, justified or not, orderly or not, yell police brutality—if it does not happen, provoke it by foul language, physical abuse, whatever, and then count on a larger measure of sympathy from the up-to-now apathetic or passive members of the community. Then call for amnesty, the head of the president on a platter, the complete submission to any and all demands. One beleaguered president has said that these people want to be martyrs thrown to toothless lions. He added, "Who wants to dialogue when they are going for the jugular vein?"

So it has gone, and it is generally well orchestrated. Again, my only question: Must it be so? Must universities be subjected, willy-nilly, to such intimidation and victimization whatever their good will in the matter? Somewhere a stand must be made.

I only ask that when the stand is made necessary by those who would destroy the community and all its basic yearning for great and calm educational opportunity, let them carry the blame and the penalty. No one wants the forces of law on this or any other campus, but if some necessitate it, as a last and dismal alternative to anarchy and mob tyranny, let them shoulder the blame instead of receiving the sympathy of a community they would hold at bay. The only alternative I can imagine is turning the majority of the community loose on them, and then you have two mobs. I know of no one who would opt for this alternative—always lurking in the wings. We can have a thousand resolutions as to what kind of a society we want, but when lawlessness is afoot, and all authority is flouted, faculty, administration, and student, then we invoke the normal societal forces of law or we allow the university to die beneath our hapless and hopeless gaze. I have no intention of presiding over such a spectacle: too many people have given too much of themselves and their lives to this university to let this happen here. Without being melodramatic, if this conviction makes this my last will and testament to Notre Dame, so be it.

May I now say in all sincerity that I never want to see any student expelled from this community because, in many ways, this is always an educative failure. Even so, I must likewise be committed to the survival of the university community as one of man's best hopes in these troubled times. I know of no other way of insuring both ends than to say of every member of this community, faculty and students, that we are all ready and prepared and anxious to respond to every intellectual and moral concern in the world today, in every way proper to the university. At the same time, we cannot allow a small minority to impose their will on the majority who have spoken regarding the university's style of life; we cannot allow a few to substitute force of any kind for persuasion to accept their personal idea of what is right or proper. We only insist on the rights of all, minority and majority, the climate of civility and rationality, and a preponderant moral abhorrence of violence or inhuman forms of persuasion that violate our style of life and the nature of the university. It is, unfortunately, possible to cut oneself off from this community, even though the vast majority of our members would regret seeing it happen. However, should this occur, the community as a whole has indicated that it will vote and stand for the maintenance of this community's deepest values, since this is the price we all pay for the survival of the university community in the face of anyone and everyone who would destroy or denature it today, for whatever purposes.

May I now confess that since last November I have been bombarded mightily by the hawks and the doves—almost equally. I have resisted both and continue to recognize the right to protest— through every legitimate channel—and to resist as well those who would unthinkingly trifle with the survival of the university as one of the few open societies left to mankind today. There is no divine assurance that the university will survive as we have known and cherished it—but we do commit ourselves to make the effort and count on this community, in this place, to uphold the efforts that you have inspired by your clear expression of community concern. Thanks to all who have declared themselves, even to those who have slightly disagreed, but are substantially concerned as well.

As long as the great majority of this community is concerned and involved in maintaining what it believes deeply to be its identity and commitment, no force within it, however determined or organized, can really destroy it. If any community as a whole does not believe this, or is not committed to it, it does not deserve to survive and it probably will not. I hope we will. To this, I commit myself with the presumption that the great majority of you are with me in this concern and commitment.

I truly believe that we are about to witness a revulsion on the part of legislatures, state and national, benefactors, parents, alumni, and the general public for much that is happening in higher education today. If I read the signs of the times correctly, this may well lead to a suppression of the liberty and autonomy that are the lifeblood of a university community. It may well lead to a rebirth of fascism, unless we ourselves are ready to take a stand for what is right for us. History is not consoling in this regard. We rule ourselves or others rule us, in a way that destroys the university as we have known and loved it.

Devotedly yours in Notre Dame,

(Rev.) Theodore M. Hesburgh, C.S.C.
President

Bogotá, Columbia
February 27, 1969

Dear Mr. Vice-President:

President Nixon has asked me to give you my views regarding campus unrest and possible action on the occasion of your meeting this week with the governors of the fifty states. The President most wisely states that any action must be "consistent with the vital importance of maintaining the traditional independence of American universities." In the concluding sentence of my recent letter to Notre Dame faculty and students I voiced my own central concern in the face of our current crisis: "We rule ourselves, or others rule us, in a way that destroys the university as we have known and loved it."

Universities, like countries, can be equally destroyed from inside or from outside. The motivation may be different, to hurt or to help, but the result is the same—no more university: mob rule instead of civility, force substituting for reason, tyranny for persuasion, police state instead of the house of the intellect with all its glorious virtues exercised in freedom.

Writing from such a distance and in the midst of a busy conference, I shall make my comments as brief as possible.

1. The best salvation for the university in the face of any crisis is for
   the university community to save itself, by declaring its own
   ground rules and basic values and then enforcing them with the
   widest and deepest form of moral persuasion for the good life of
   the university, and consequent moral condemnation with
   academic sanctions for any movement against university life and
   values—especially violence, vandalism, and mob action, which
   are the antitheses of reason, civility, and the open society which
   respects the rights of each and all.

2. When moral persuasion and academic sanctions fail to deter
   those who show open contempt for the life-style and self-
   declared values of the university community, there should be no
   hesitation to invoke whatever outside assistance is necessary to
   preserve the university and its values. However, it is the university that best judges its need for outside assistance and invokes
   this assistance, much as it would call for help in a three-alarm
   campus fire. Here the concern is survival against forces bent on
   destruction.

3. It is important to see and judge universities today as they really
   are, not as they appear to be. The bizarre and widely publicized
   antics of relatively few students and relatively even fewer faculty
   are accepted as the stereotypes of all students and all faculty,
   much to the disgust of this widely maligned majority of faculty
   and students. The vast majority of university and college students today are a very promising and highly attractive group of
   persons: they are more informed, more widely read, better educated, more idealistic and more deeply sensitive to crucial moral
   issues in our times, more likely to dedicate themselves to good
   rather than selfish goals than any past generation of students I
   have known. Many of them are bothered by some aspects of
   American and world society and current values or the lack of
   them—with good reason in most cases. They would work very
   hard, I believe, if given a real opportunity to participate in changing this world for the better. They would also find out how hard
   this is to do and would quickly discard some of their more naive
   present solutions to our problems. Even then most far-out stu-

dents are trying to tell society something that may also be worth searching for today if they would only lower the volume so we could hear the message. Anyway, the great majority of our students need better leadership than we or the faculty have been giving them. In a fast-changing society the real crisis is not one of authority but a crisis of vision that alone can inspire great leadership and create great morale in any society. A rebirth of great academic, civic and political leadership, a sharing of some of these youthful ideals and dreams (impossible or not) would be good for our universities and good for America too. It might also help us all remove some of the key problems that underlie most of the unrest. The campus is really reflecting America and the world today in hi-fi sound and living color.

4. Part of the vision I have been speaking of must certainly include law and order. But curiously enough, one cannot really have law and order without another part of the vision: greater achievement of justice in our times, more compassion for all, real love between generations. All elements of the vision are interdependent. Moreover, the vision must be whole and real for everyone. Lastly, a measure of humor would help from time to time to break up the deathly seriousness of the present scene.

5. As to present action: I would make the following two suggestions:

A. Assume for a few months that the university community—faculty, students, administration, and trustees—is capable, in most cases, of laying down its own guidelines and effectively maintaining them in its usual free and independent university style. Things will be messy from time to time, but we will make it as universities if we determine strongly to maintain our freedoms and our values. That determination is growing on every campus, every day now. Give it elbow room in which to grow and operate in its own good way.

B. Where special help is needed, let all assume it will be asked for and given quickly, effectively, and as humanely as possible, given the provocations that surround the need for such outside help, as a last alternative to internal self-correction. But let it be understood that the university, and only the university, public or private, makes this determination.

If my two assumptions are correct, the crisis will pass without the further requirement of actions other than those contained in my assumptions, especially not repressive legislation, or overreaction in its many forms.

May I conclude with a word of optimism? As Dickens wrote in *A Tale of Two Cities*, "It was the best of times; it was the worst of times." The worst, because many of our best traditions, as universities and as a nation, are under siege. The best of times, because we are going to win the battle, not by repressing the very values of rationality, civility, and openness that we are trying to save, but by reinforcing them in our belief, in our lives, in our institutions, and especially by using them, and, hopefully, youth's great vigor and idealism as well, to attack the deeper problems yet ahead of us in our agelong walk out of the jungle into the light.

My best personal regards, and prayers too, for you, Mr. Vice-President, and all the governors.

Devotedly yours,

Rev. Theodore M. Hesburgh, C.S.C.
President
University of Notre Dame

SECTION FIVE

The Future:
Church, Education, World

In these last chapters, I thought it might be well to take a look at the future, after having examined the past and the present.

The first chapter was an address given to the national convention of the Catholic Press Association in 1974, a time when the aftereffects of Vatican Council II, which had ended in 1965, were still seen in the opening up of a church glacially stable and closed during the four-and-a-half centuries following the Reformation. The Council's influence on the relationship of the church and Catholic higher education was mainly for the good. While the church in America supports and largely controls parochial elementary and secondary education, albeit in a most decentralized fashion, many people do not realize that Catholic colleges and universities are not chartered or controlled or even financially supported by the authorities of the church, the hierarchy. People are surprised when I tell them Notre Dame has not received a nickel of support from the institutional church for more than a century. They are further surprised when I tell them Notre Dame is held in public trust by a board of some forty persons, only seven of whom are clerics, the rest laypersons, not all Catholics.

The second chapter was written for a book published by Change Magazine Press and forecasts what higher education might look like in the year 2000. If my guesses are wrong, at least I shall not have to defend them. Even so, I hope they are right, because I continue to be an optimist.

The third chapter, which explores the implications of interdependence on a global scale, looks to the future of the planet earth itself and came about because I was called upon one day in 1974 at the university by a distinguished Englishman, Sir Michael Stewart. He had come many miles to ask me to deliver an address; most people do the same by a telephone call. It was difficult to say no to his request: to deliver the annual lecture at Ditchley Manor near Oxford University.

This, I knew, was a distinguished lecture series. I decided to speak on an idea that had been gnawing at me for some months: interdependence. We Americans have been brought up on the notion of independence. Interdependence is quite the opposite. It seemed to me to say in one word just exactly where we were at this historical moment in the world's history. I will let the essay speak for itself, but it did seem to be a new and bright and most important idea at the time, even though, like all good ideas that catch on as this one did, the word has been terribly overworked since then. I still think that it is a key and very important idea for understanding today's world and for formulating an agenda to cure its ills in all the days ahead.

XVI

The Post–Vatican II Church

One of our alumni recently asked me: Where is the church going? What will it be like when my children are my age? I have found over the years that our alumni often ask questions like this, seemingly simple, yet requiring a great deal of thought to answer adequately. I do not remember what I answered on the spur of the moment, but it could not have been spectacular. Yet, I did remember the question and would like to try to answer it in a more leisurely and more thoughtful fashion now. I speak, of course, of the Catholic Church, since I know that best.

As we approach the next millennium, futurology, the science of the future, has become a familiar academic pastime. Many books are appearing here and in Europe with the magic year number 2000 in their titles. Even I have contributed one in the form of the Terry Lectures at Yale University.

However, most of this futurology deals with the secular world of economic, social, political, scientific, and technological changes. There is very little speculation on the future of the church or the churches in these books.

It does not take much imagination or information to see that in a rapidly changing world, the churches are changing, too, and especially the Catholic Church, due particularly to the effects of Vatican Council II. In many ways, the Catholic Church had been the great unchanged and unchanging reality in the modern world of the twentieth century. The Protestant churches had been changing and evolving in many ways since the Reformation, four-and-a-half centuries ago. But during these centuries, the Catholic Church stood on dead center, and I use the adjective advisedly, since change—at least in nonessentials—is a condition of life and growth. It is fair to say that there has been more change in the church during the last 10 years than during the preceding 450 years. Some of the change, in fact, most of it, was good and needed. Some few of the changes, or what accompanied the changes, were silly phenomena that will, I trust, soon become passé and forgotten, as other secular fads, like the hula hoop, come and go without any lasting effect.

However, there were changes that were radical, fundamental, even, for the church, revolutionary. These changes will necessarily affect the whole future evolution of the church, both short-range and long-range. We have been living with the short-range effects and can more easily describe and, hopefully, understand them. As to the long-range effects, we can only speculate and hope.

Among the most basic of the changes in the church that emerged from Vatican Council II was what, for want of a better word, I would simply call "openness." Having read practically all the journalistic books that appeared during and after the Council, I believe that one of the best was Michael Novak's *The Open Church*. Perhaps it is his analysis that influences my choice of the word "openness." Michael Novak once explained what he meant by the adjective "open":

> By "open," I did not mean permissive, or flaccid, or noncommittal—as in the phrase "open marriage." I had in mind the image of inquiring intellect, disciplined by concrete fact (in insight) and by evidence (in judgment)— "open" to the demands of inquiry, but "closed," too, by the exigencies of inquiry. I did not imagine that "anything goes."
>
> But by "open," the contemporary temper, particularly in America, frequently seems to mean "without limits," "without negatives," "without demands." In the name of

transcendence, barbarism is cultivated. "Liberation" seldom means the acceptance of responsibilities, duties, and limits; it tends to mean doing what one pleases when one pleases; it is sometimes a synonym for infantilism, a flight from social bonds and concrete duties.

The human spirit, ironically, gains such freedom as is accessible to it by the route of interdiction; by the acceptance of limits; by the disciplines of social and institutional involvement. There is no genuine learning, for example, without the humble submission of intelligence to the demands and discipline of plodding inquiry, in community with others who do not allow one to do simply as one pleases.

I suppose that one might begin to understand this new openness in the church by looking at its opposite, which well characterizes the pre–Vatican Council II church, namely "the closed church." There will be those who quibble about my term or Novak's, saying that the church has always been open to everyone. This objection really reinforces the difference because the church was open indeed, but only on its own terms. To enter, you had to come home and leave all your baggage behind you.

When I grew up, the church had all the answers to every conceivable question and the answers were always black and white. We were right and everyone else was wrong. There was no partial truth, no tentative searching, no intellectual modesty—the leadership simply said yes or no, right or wrong, and that was that. Authority was a force to be reckoned with in the closed church. The reckoning was simple: authority commanded and you obeyed; no questions asked; no reasons given; only the statement, "You do it because I say do it; do it or get out."

I am, of course, speaking somewhat in caricature, but certainly not altogether so. If even the state wanted to progress, it had better listen to the church's advice, since we also had the last word of wisdom to say about political as well as economic and social reality. If there was evil in these secular worlds of politics, business, or societal life, it was because they were not listening carefully enough to what the church, the perfect society, was saying. If culture was degenerating, again the church could give the reason why. Evil books, that is, evil in the church's judgment, were put on the Index, not to be read by faithful Christians without special permission, even in the university. The church would tell you what movies to see or not to see as well. Again, these judgments, aesthetic and intellectual as well as moral, were made peremptorily, finally, with unfailing certitude and enforced rigidly up and down the line. When you said church, you meant everyone from the pope to the parish janitor or the head of the Altar and Rosary Society. Everyone's style was the same, from top to bottom: authoritarian, unyielding, righteous, unquestioning, or, if described less lovingly from the outside, cocksure.

This was the salient character of the church I knew for most of the years of my life, the church I learned about at home, at school, in the parish, especially in the seminary. It was surely a law and order church. It was growing larger numerically, even if along rigid lines. There was little doubt expressed. What few revolts occurred were dealt with effectively and quickly—out you go. It was peaceful in a way, superobedient and faithful, easy to govern, and for all of these reasons, triumphalistic in style, medieval monarchic in governance, as safe and secure as the gilt-edged government bonds of the time, and about as exciting as a graveyard in its easy victory over the world of the flesh and the devil.

Then along came a man named John who opened the windows to let in the fresh air of modern reality. One can argue whether he really knew what he was doing, but certainly the Holy Spirit knew and Pope John did listen well. Earlier popes had written beautiful treatises about just wages. John did not write. He just doubled the unjust wages paid everyone at the Vatican. His simple deed spoke louder than all the beautiful words of his predecessors.

By opening Vatican Council II, Pope John, in fact, opened the church. He also opened it to the other Christian churches which had not even been called churches before. He opened it to non-Christians, even welcomed discussions with non-believers and remarked to Khrushchev's daughter that her son's name was the same as his, and could he pray especially for little Ivan? John opened the church to freedom of conscience. His Council discarded the ancient chestnut that "error has no rights," since rights inhere in human persons, whether or not in error, and not in abstractions like the notion of error. John opened the church to great theologians who had been abruptly silenced before. He welcomed new ideas from whatever source, apologized to the Jews for centuries of anti-Semitism, declaring with open arms, "I am Joseph [his baptismal name], your brother." John recognized that, in fact, the world was not waiting with bated breath for every declaration from a triumphalistic church or pontifical churchmen. He introduced modesty, receptiveness, listening, in a word, openness.

In a very real sense, after John XXIII died, Pope Paul VI has had to pick up the pieces, to restore some semblance of order to the church through which the winds of change, pent up for almost five centuries, had been blowing with hurricane force during Pope John's brief pontificate. It is unfortunately, but inevitably, the quite unfair task for our age to try to assimilate in a decade or two the whole world of change that should have been taking place slowly, gradually, and organically, over the past five centuries.

I suspect that central to our problem today is that the leadership of the church was formed, trained, and accustomed to govern the safe, sane, and secure church of pre–Vatican Council II. Methods of governance that were perfect then are disastrous now. Attitudes, mind-sets, frames of reference, modes of thought and discourse that worked well then, a short time ago, do not work at all today, in fact, are often counterproductive. Habits born of centuries of sailing in halcyon waters do not prepare either the officers or the crew to sail through a sudden and unexpected hurricane with gale-force winds and mountainous waves. Every normal action now must become an unprecedented improvisation. I am somewhat reminded of the world revolution we encountered in the university world in the late sixties.

The difference between the universities and the church is that in the universities, the leadership was largely swept out when hard times came, and the leaders were replaced by those who had proved themselves adept at crisis management, mostly younger men. In the church, the leadership is practically for life.

If the officers of Peter's Barque are having trouble, you can be sure that the crew is troubled, too. Never before in the church's long history have so many of the officers and crew jumped ship. Again, one must try to understand and to be compassionate, even while welcoming and applauding the changes that caused all this insecurity. The pre–Vatican II church, as described above, was so highly structured, so authoritarian and secure, that one could literally lean on the walls and the walls would support all who leaned. There were many who leaned, rather than stand on their own two feet. When authority was first questioned, and showed its feet of clay, when the secure walls began to shake and some of them fell, many people who were leaning on those walls fell with them.

People used to total support, total security, absolute answers to everything, find it hard, if not impossible, to survive in a growing atmosphere of insecurity, reasonable doubt, questioning, and openness. Every crisis, every cataclysmic change has its predictable casualties—those who cannot change, who cannot adjust to the new reality. We all have to regret this in the church, but we also have to recognize that the crisis had to come sooner or later, and the hour was already very late for the inevitable change. Now that it has happened, we must do all we can to help those who were hurt, who still cannot understand, but that is not a reason for turning back the clock, for attempting to reverse the normal flow of history.

If kindness and understanding for former bishops, priests, nuns, and disaffected Catholics is part of the price we pay, it is even more a demand of simple Christian charity in our times. Love for our brethren and sisters needs no justification or explanation. We need to grant understanding and love as well to those at both ends of the spectrum within the church, those ultraconservatives who cannot live comfortably with the changes, and those ultraliberals who want to change everything that is yet unchanged, whether or not it is good or proper or even useful to change it.

Both groups should, I believe, be lived with in whatever peace can be managed during this necessarily interim period. If one group wants a Latin, old-style Mass for themselves (or for their burial, as one old friend has prescribed), so be it, and why not? If the other group wants quite awful music and somewhat vulgar ceremonies for one of their celebrations, we should swallow our ancient instinctive anathemas and suffer it—in the belief that bad music and cheapness die of their own inadequacy in time. If the Pentecostals, somewhere along this spectrum, have their own preferred way, why not let them have the benefit of the Gamaliel principle: "If this movement of theirs is of human origin, it will break up of its own accord; but if it does, in fact, come from God, you will not only be unable to destroy them, but you might find yourselves fighting against God."

We should have no less love for those who have left the church altogether, so they think, either because it has changed too much or not enough. Again, they are casualties of a crisis and we should emulate God's understanding, as well as his love and mercy for all. We may well need the same love and mercy ourselves some day.

Thus far, I have been attempting to analyze and describe what has been happening in the church recently, rather than speculating in answer to the Notre Dame alumnus's question as to where we are going in the years ahead. I have not been avoiding the answer, but laying the foundation for it. One cannot speculate about the future with any assurance unless he understands something of the past and present, where we have been and where we seem to be right now, or, in the awful jargon of the day, "seeing where it's at, letting it all hang out." Having done just that, however cursorily and in shorthand, now we shall look ahead.

Here are some definite predictions for the church in the future, based on dynamisms already in being and at work. I claim no special wisdom or foresight, just enormous interest and concern.

"Openness" will continue to characterize, more and more,

the postconciliar church. There will, of course, be counter-movements, nostalgia for a more serene and settled past, the constant drag of ultraconservatism from authoritarians, but the flow of history will not be reversed: no more Index; no more Holy Office and modern Inquisition; no more suppression of university theologians who speculate on the frontiers of theology; no more quiet exiles for those who dare to question; no more secret and hidden agenda of the powerful clerical few; no more triumphalistic lording it over other Christian communities; no more arrogance of "our" truth or suppression of "their" error; no more unconcern for a vast world formerly labeled heathen or pagan; no more disdain for insights from a world formerly called profane; no more seeming to control, for our own purposes, Our Lord and Savior's grace or the Holy Spirit's movement; no more pretense of having the ultimate answer to every question; no more inhumanity of canon law applied like Roman civil law before Christianity changed that world; no more insensitivity to immense problems like poverty, population, racism, global justice; no more one-man rule on every level of authority; no more unconscious assumption that the church is a male preserve, or a Roman one either; no more unconcern for the voice and presence and will of the people of God in the church, which is to say, the laity. Again, such lists tend to caricature reality, but there is no item I have mentioned without its own historical reality in the past. The overriding of all of this dismal reality is precisely what Popes John and Paul accomplished by inaugurating the Council and bringing it to a successful conclusion. It was not so much the vast production of documents that changed and is changing the church, but the vital tension of the debate that preceded their writing and the prophetic spirit that voted their passage and has continued to be concerned with their implementation, despite growing opposition.

Openness is here to stay, thank God, and the church is much better because of this fundamental change. The church is not more secure, safer, more peaceful, more orderly, but it is more modest and less triumphant; more Christlike and less worldly and wealthy; more conscious of its central apostolic mission and less cluttered by interference in secular affairs that are none of its business; more involved in the world's growing problems of justice and peace and less immersed in politics; more concerned with ecumenical "oneness in Christ" and less conscious about others finding us; more ready to learn, less sure of teaching everyone, everything; more ready to serve than to control others; praying for forgiveness for ourselves and pardoning all others; more totally dedicated to Christ and his Kingdom; more open to the Spirit—the most fundamental openness of all.

The church of the future will be more decentralized in every way, from the new collegial structures of the Vatican to the moral weight placed upon the informed individual conscience of the lay Christian. The gradually changing leadership of the church, from top to bottom, will be ever more conscious of the collegial mode of governance on every level; of the importance of hanging loose, of not solving every problem the day it occurs, not having a definitive answer for every question, not judging too quickly, depending more upon the Holy Spirit and his inspiration to guide the church through these difficult days.

Leaders will learn increasingly that to lead in the church, they will need for their personal credibility more than the simple fact of having been appointed to an office by a distant authority. They will often have to establish personal credibility after their appointment by the continual moral stature of their lives, actions, judgments. No more will our country indulge in a century of unbridled racism without strong words and actions from religious leaders. No more will an immoral war go uncriticized for the most part by official religious leaders until it has been condemned by almost everyone else. No more will world poverty be of no concern as long as we are affluent.

Our moral indignation can no longer be selective either, if moral credibility is to be established. We cannot be loud in condemning abortion after being silent about napalmed Vietnamese children or seemingly unconscious of the horrible present fact that 50 percent of the children already born in the poorest countries, with more than a billion inhabitants, die before the age of five. We can and must do something about abortion, but it must be one of several equally horrendous problems that we are doing something about. It must not be booked as a Catholic problem either; it is a human problem.

Leadership in the church will, I believe, be not only generally more decentralized and collegial in the future, but also less official. In times of great change, leadership is where you find it. This is especially true of moral and spiritual leadership. I would expect to see more varied leadership in the church in the future, more leadership from religious brothers and sisters (a particularly underemployed source of great talent) and, of course, more leadership on the part of laymen and laywomen, who will begin to understand in an increasingly decentralized and declericalized future that they do not just belong to the church, but that they are the greatest part of what the church is, the people of God. Contrast this reality with the number of articles on *de clericis* and *de laicis* in the Code of Canon Law. As one who wrote his doctoral thesis thirty years ago on "The Theology of the Laity," I am delighted to see this new development, this new openness to leadership from all quarters in the church.

I would hope that the church of the years ahead would be less polarized than the church of today, more concerned about substantive religious problems and less divided over peripheral issues. The language of the liturgy, the mode of receiving Holy Communion, the kinds of sticky problems that we openly discuss on university campuses, these are all much less important in themselves than praying well together in a meaningful liturgy, receiving the Lord with love and devotion and delight, being willing to meet and discuss with civility and courtesy any of the great moral issues that divide us from our fellow citizens. Even worse than not discussing problems is to be divided on nonproblems that do not deserve our time, attention, or energy. There is nothing worse than Christians abusing and name-calling each other, destroying Christian peace and unity in Christ, fomenting division, distrust, and malice.

I really expect that there will be one Christian Church in the years ahead, one characterized by unity, but not by uniformity. It is possible to imagine a union of all Christians in the faith, together with a variety of liturgies and communities such as already exist within the Catholic and Protestant and Orthodox churches. Even the papacy is no longer an insurmountable obstacle with the advent of collegiality and the acknowledged need for a center of Christian unity, a strong voice for spiritual and moral concern. *Petrus redivivus.*

It must be said that for the moment, despite the yearnings of Christians, the official ecumenical movement is moving at snail's pace. But we tend to forget the high plateau that was attained by Protestants, Orthodox, and Catholics so quickly and seemingly so easily, like an idea whose time had come. Suddenly, during and after the Council, the ancient antagonisms faded away, to be replaced by understanding and cooperation.

It is practically unthinkable that the internecine warfare with all its confessional horrors will ever be renewed again. The official conversations between and among various Protestant and Catholic churches have made some progress, but the going is slow. In fact, the ecumenical movement seems to be making more progress unofficially today than in the context of the ecclesiastical establishments. Many Christians pray together and instinctively communicate together in each other's churches, whatever the official view of this. I am not passing judgment, but remarking on what is already happening. Young people, particularly, are much more concerned about all that unites them in faith than in what separates them for a variety of lesser political or historical reasons.

No one can say when or how Christian unity will finally come in the days ahead. Possibly one day the reality will be there demanding recognition. Maybe it will just happen in general practice, before or during the theoretical discussions. Conceivably, some great global crisis will bring unity in fact. Since the good Lord, who promised us that all prayer is heard, did in fact himself pray for this oneness during his last night on earth, might we not hope that it will come to pass soon in the days ahead?

I expect to see considerably more political action on the part of Catholics in the future. In the past, Catholic laymen and laywomen in the church were said to be those who prayed and paid and obeyed. In the state, it was not all that different. Catholics were among the most patriotic of Americans. They faithfully paid all their taxes, kept the law, served in the Armed Forces, died generously for their country in every war, did much of America's dirty work—dug the canals, built the railroads and highways, manned the industrial revolution, bought and paid for their modest homes, supported their church, and educated their children in their own patriotic and religious context. They did not ask a great deal from America, but they were victimized for a while for their religion and later proved it could help them be the best of citizens and patriots. Meanwhile, they grew in numbers, but did not use their strength for special favors. Now they number 50 million, about a fourth of all Americans.

Lately, I have perceived some stirrings among these quiet, faithful, patriotic, modest American Catholics. They are beginning to feel set upon, ignored, even badly used and unappreciated. Let me illustrate from past happenings. In 1968, 50 million American Catholics wanted two things: first, some help—even modest—to the parochial schools that educated many of their children as they desired; and second, no liberalization of the laws on abortion. What happened? The Catholics were denied help to parochial schools and abortion was made legal practically on demand for any reason. Even I am upset when my own brother says he could today get a tax credit if he paid for an abortion, but not for the considerable expenses he pays for his children's attendance at three different Catholic schools.

Nineteen sixty-eight is 1968, but memories remain. The next time, I expect that Catholics will have better leadership, will be more highly politicized, more conscious of their inherent strength, less ready to be promised help by a president who, once he had their votes, hardly lifted a finger to help them or their two causes.

The future will also see Catholic scholars, having proved their worth in the Council, ready and willing to work with the bishops for the total good and growth of the church. No longer can the church afford the luxury of unused human resources. There need be no tension between the two groups of leaders, in the hierarchy and in the universities. They may well be operating on a different set of tracks, but there are multiple areas today where the tracks converge, particularly in the areas of social justice, human development, medical ethics, culture and the arts, political action, and continuing education. As Bishop James Rausch, the former spokesman for the United States bishops, put it, "If there is any single issue which requires attention, it is indispensable cooperation between Catholic scholars and bishops." Here is an idea whose time has really come.

May I conclude with one last personal note. Whatever the actual state of the church in the future, and whatever our basic agreements or disagreements about what might and should come to pass, at least might we all face the future together in faith, hope, and love. These are the virtues that guide us Godward and the only virtues that can help us guide the future Godward.

I recently read through Philip Hughes's version of twenty centuries of church history. It was incredible how low the church sank on occasion, and how high it rose in other times. The peaks and valleys succeeded each other through the long centuries, and there never was a time when it was all peak or all valley. Saints lived in the worst of times, and great sinners in the best of times. It seems to me that we should now leave this present time unjudged as better or worse, being grateful for the holy ones we have with us, the good leaders wherever they emerge, the great inspirations, the quiet heroes and heroines, the high hopes and the roads leading to them. Let us only move ahead into the future with faith and hope and love—knowing that the church will somehow survive as it always has, as has been promised by the Lord himself. But beyond survival, let us strain to catch a glimpse of a peak up ahead and let us press onward whenever the path, however uncertain, seems to lead upward.

XVII

Education
in the Year 2000

If prophesy one must, and it is a chancy business at best given the paucity of authentic prophets, the millennial year just ahead of us will probably find everyone prophesying. We have only had one other millennial year, 1000, in this Christian era. At that time, there were dire predictions of the end of the world, wild chiliastic dreams, doomsday coming, and all the rest. We will probably hear it again. One would hope that we have matured during the present millennium. Certainly, the world is vastly different than it was in the year 1000. No one would have been discussing the future of higher education then, because they were still two hundred years away from the founding of the first university in Paris. Intellectually, the ages then were dark at best, the language mainly a bastard Latin, the manuscripts few in that pre-Gutenberg age. By our standards, almost everyone, except a few clerics, was illiterate, life was culturally brutal, learning almost nonexistent, except for the preservation in the monasteries of a few intellectual gems of a long-distant golden age. I speak of the Western world, the only world celebrating this particular millennium, although for our humility, it should be mentioned that there were a few bright lights glowing in Asia and, strangely enough, in Meso-America. Despite the new and different kind of gloom that characterizes our age, unlike those prophets of a thousand years ago, crouched over a flickering candle in the mountain vastness of Subiaco or Monte Cassino, I, a kind of monk like them, at least sharing their common vows of poverty, chastity, and obedience, write these lines on a yellow pad instead of parchment, with a ball point instead of a feather pen, not in a monastery, but higher than they in their mountains, traveling at 600 miles an hour in the bright clear air at 37,000 feet above the Atlantic, midway between Europe and America.

Despite the incredible change of pace in the conditions surrounding us, now as compared to then, life and learning fundamentally pose some of the same problems. They are mainly orientational problems of value, meaning, direction, attitude, ultimately salvation now and eternally for the many who still believe in eternity, however incoherently, no less longingly.

While the year 2000 will likely bring some changes in the human condition, I would not see anything cataclysmic, barring nuclear or biological warfare. We will probably muck up the world somewhat more, but less rapidly than at present. There will be a few more billion people aboard our spacecraft, but again they will be mostly on the other side of the globe and in the Southern Hemisphere. Again, the rate of growth will have begun to level off, if we will have had enough sense to have helped them develop more humanly than at present. There will be scientific breakthroughs, though nothing as spectacular as nuclear energy, rocketry, computers, and all that they made possible in the last quarter-century. Our future scientific gains will be more generally in the field of biology than in chemistry and physics, although the great gains in these latter will have facilitated the biological spectaculars yet to come. I doubt that we will have heard from other intelligent beings in the universe by the year 2000, although I have no doubt that they are there.

Against this background, it may sound banal to predict a few modest changes in the world of higher education, specifically in the United States, which happens to be the world leader in this field.

First, I suspect that we will struggle to strike a better balance between equality and quality than exists at present. As a member of both the Commission on Civil Rights and the Carnegie Commission on the Future of Higher Education, I pressed long and fervently for better access to higher education on the part of those minorities so long denied equality of opportunity. While the task is still unfinished, we have succeeded beyond our initial hopes, and the machinery is in place for further success. As so often happens in human affairs, the good was in some way the enemy of the better. Equality often came at the cost of quality, funds for the latter being transferred to the former. Quality of education was also wounded in more subtle ways. Greater masses of minorities were given what often was called higher education, but really was not. This is understandable, since a decade cannot make up for the deficiencies of centuries. However, I would predict that wiser counsel and greater balance will prevail by the year 2000. Equality is essential to our political system and moral convictions as a nation. Yet, without the highest quality of learning as a constant standard, supported concurrently and generously with equality, the higher learning will sink ever lower, to the dismal level of the least common denominator. As the leader in higher education in all the world, we cannot debase its value, even while we widen access to higher education. I look for a growing balance in that equation, hopefully reaching equilibrium by the year 2000, if not before. Prophecy here brings a dire warning—if we do not cherish quality of education and the highest educational standards, we will have given equal access to that which is really not worth having, because without high quality, education is a counterfeit and a fraud.

Secondly, I believe that higher learning in the year 2000 will be more closely and finely focused on how to learn continually. If anything impresses one comparing the world of the year 1000 to that of 2000, it is the enormous growth in what now must be learned, the rate of growth with which we must cope in the learning process. I suspect the learning of the future will strike the note of intellectual curiosity, anticipation of what is yet to come, rather than simple control of present knowledge, security in the current state of the art. In the future, even starting today, students must learn to live with rapid, abrupt, and even frightening change. Learning will be correlative with life, an exciting intellectual adventure for which students will have to be explicitly prepared.

Thirdly, I voice a hope as much as a prophecy. In a world of sudden and cataclysmic change, simple sanity requires some constants. Navigation requires some reasonably fixed points of reference. Without navigation, life today becomes irrational wandering, a journey with no homecoming, a voyage without a port of call, a story without meaning or ending.

Higher education in our day is weakest in this respect. Values, whether intellectual or moral, are largely characterized by their absence. Often enough, we cannot even agree on what these values should be as constants, much less how they might possibly be part of higher education. One would hope that between now and the year 2000 we might, as a means of intellectual and moral survival, begin to renew in higher education the kind of dialogue that sought a higher learning in Plato's *Republic*; in Aristotle's *Ethics*; in the Old and New Testaments; in the history of saints and sinners, heroes and cowards; in the literature that so beautifully has personalized values or the lack of them in recent centuries. We should not be afraid to seek wisdom and virtue in other cultures than our own, for greatness and goodness are humanly great and good wherever they are found. They are the constants that bring quality to the whole endeavor of higher education, to the life and achievement of humankind in every age. Somehow in the welter and abruptness of change, we have lost our grip on these constants. We would all admit in the quiet of our consciences that justice is better than injustice, love better than hate, integrity better than dishonesty, compassion better than insensitivity, beauty better than ugliness, hope better than despair, faith better than infidelity, order better than chaos, peace better than war, life better than death, knowledge better than ignorance, and so on and on and on.

All these are constants that were important to the monk on the mountain and the peasant in the field in the year 1000. Whatever the enormity of our growth in knowledge and technique since then, they are still important for all of us today. We will be neither educated, nor wise, nor even able to cope with change, to navigate through life, without these constants, these values. As change heightens, as indeed it will, I would hope that higher education will include for everyone a long and longing look at these values, as a measure of what we are or are not becoming as a people, a nation, a world.

Lastly, I prophesy that higher education in the year 2000 will challenge its students to create a rather new kind of world, characterized by quite different social, economic, and political arrangements. The emphasis will be on the interdependence of nation states. Students will be challenged to be world citizens as they seek solutions to problems of human rights, ecumenism, food, fuel, shelter, health care, urbanization, pollution, crime, terrorism, development, education. None of these problems has a purely national solution. They are all illustrative of the interdependence of all humankind today. No longer can geographic prejudice decree that being born in the Northern Hemisphere promises an infinitely more human and humane existence than being born in the Southern part of spaceship earth. No longer can the affluent and powerful view the world as if everything important runs on a line between New York, London, Paris, Moscow, and Tokyo. Better than two-thirds of humanity lives well south of that line and it is their earth, too. Students in the year 2000 will increasingly be made conscious of the possibility of creating a better world than the one they are inheriting, one with liberty and justice for all, not just Americans, with liberty, equality, and fraternity for all, not just Frenchmen.

Since we do not live well or even perform well in the face of abrupt discontinuities, one might hope that the value of a world view characterized by the interdependence of all humankind might begin to enter into the substance of higher education even now, so that the year 2000 will be a crescendo of interdependence, not a belated beginning. This would then become a self-fulfilling prophecy.

The real value of looking ahead, even prophesying, is that it clarifies our present perspectives and priorities and hopes. It has been said that a journey of a thousand miles begins with one step. Before taking that step into the future, it is good to know where this first step leads us, so that our goal becomes our prophecy as we walk with hope and vision, even today.

XVIII

Problems and Opportunities on a Very Interdependent Planet

Interdependence is a thought and a theme that runs counter to many of our shibboleths of the past: nationalism, ethnocentrism, rugged individualism, empire, cold war, East and West with never the twain meeting, declarations of independence. How did interdependence so suddenly emerge as an idea whose time has come? Partially, I believe, it came as a response to new and unprecedented challenges that have burst upon the world scene in recent years. More fundamentally, it represents a kind of modern Copernican revolution that involves a new way of looking at our world. I have been impressed by the fact that this new look is a fallout of the space age, whose most important result was not close-up pictures of the moon, but a new look at the world from afar. There it whirls in the black void of space, blue and brown, flecked with white clouds, in the words of Lady Jackson, Barbara Ward, our "Spaceship Earth."

When asked what impressed him most in viewing the earth from the moon, one astronaut said: "I could put up my thumb and blot out the whole earth." Viewed as a small spacecraft, the passengers as crew, it is not a large step to understand their interdependence in all they do, living together interdependently on a planet with limited resources and growing needs. In fact, there are few serious human problems today whose impact and significance are not global, requiring, therefore, a global solution as well. I offer a small list: war and

peace, human development, population, food, energy, un-
employment, trade and commerce, communications, crime,
arms control, drugs, environment, literacy, the use of the
seas, the resources of the seabed, atomic technology, monetary systems, agriculture, air and sea transport, health.

In every one of these items, global considerations are
needed to describe their full reality, and in each of them, we
have a concrete example of the modern interdependence of
nations and mankind globally. In the past, each of these
problems or opportunities would have been viewed solely in
the national or local perspective. Today, any local or national
response to any one of these realities would be both in-
adequate and largely useless.

Take the global food problem. It is present, urgent, and
itself interdependent upon other global problems, such as
human rights, development, population, fuel, pollution, agriculture, trade, monetary balance, and a host of others relating totally to the future of life on this planet.

Our food situation has never been more precarious than at
present. Food was, of course, the almost total concern for
primitive man, so much so that early man is characterized as a
hunter or a gatherer, but never before has the whole matter of
sufficient food for survival been cast in such monumental
world proportions as at present. Food demand is up 50 percent since twenty years ago, while world food stocks have
been depleted. Climatic change has complicated the situation
by having a disastrous effect on food production. A few years
ago, I visited some of the Sahelian countries in Africa where
the Sahara Desert is moving south at about thirty miles a year.
In the refugee camps around Nouakchott, Timbuktu, and
Gao, I saw hundreds of thousands of Tuaregs who have lost
all of their herds and are despondently dependent on a minimal amount of rice, wheat, and corn flown in daily on military
airlifts. It was like attempting to feed an elephant with a
teaspoon. In those incredibly torrid and sandy spots, one sees
the face of hungry desperation and realizes that human suffering transcends the grim statistics. People starve and die, not
numbers.

As this is happening in the underdeveloped world, we in

the developed world are consuming almost a ton of food grains annually per person while the poorest barely subsist on 400 pounds a year. We only consume 150 pounds of our grain directly as bread and pastry products, the rest going into the production of meat, milk, and eggs. The poor consume all of the grain directly in bread, chapattis, and tortillas. Affluence has doubled meat consumption in recent years in America and Canada. Since it takes seven pounds of grain to produce one pound of beef, more grains are fed to animals in America than are consumed directly in the poor nations, thus further complicating the food crisis. Now the face of interdependence begins to appear. For example, a quarter of a pound less of beef a week per person in the United States would free over 10 million tons of food grains a year for a hungry world, and contribute to American health, too, with the lowering of cholesterol intake.

In the past, interdependence was seen in political terms, as the Third World was wooed by the Western and socialist countries with various assistance schemes. Now that detente has arrived among the great powers, that motivation must be replaced by a new sense of interdependence. Some call for self-interest, since we are moving into an age of shortage of industrial materials that mostly come from the Third World, oil being only the tip of the shortage iceberg. Now the banana countries, the copper producers, the bauxite group are beginning to follow the Organization of Petroleum Exporting Countries' example in forming cartels to raise prices, so they can pay for their spiraling costs of fuel and food.

These interdependent developments have given rise to a new category among the 115 countries of the Third World, namely the 35 to 40 countries who have nothing with which to bargain, neither raw materials nor industrial potential, countries such as India, Bangladesh, Sri Lanka, and Pakistan, the Sahelian countries of Africa, and some Caribbean nations. This is the new, so-called Fourth World, comprising almost a billion people.

What would interdependence suggest to the continuing food and fuel crisis for the Fourth World? We might begin by recognizing that the United States, Canada, and Australia, the only exporters of grain in the world today, are in the same relationship to the devastated Fourth World vis-à-vis food as the Organization of Petroleum Exporting Countries is regarding fuel. The least that either group could do in a truly humane and interdependent world would be to make a concessional grant of food and fuel to these countries of the Fourth World, which are now in a life-and-death position because of the rising cost of food and fuel. A long-range solution would, of course, be to aid these countries to become more self-sufficient in their own food production. Plans are available for this, but again the capital would have to come from recycling the excess profits of the surplus countries, including the oil rich countries, if the world were truly seen as interdependent. The alternative is to watch a billion people die slowly of starvation. Such recycling not only would avert that tragedy, but would also help solve the serious imbalance that threatens the world's banking, monetary, and trading systems.

As important as food inequities are disparities of population, almost half of whose net annual world addition comes from five countries, mainly in the Fourth World category— India, China, Bangladesh, Indonesia, Pakistan. We can also cite trade dominated by the twenty-four nations in the Organization of Economic Cooperation and Development, nations which consume two-thirds of the world product of $4.6 trillion, despite the fact that trade is nine times more important to the developing countries than aid, if one looks at the sheer dollar volume. The notion of interdependence, or the lack of it in practice, is illustrated by a broader look at the use of the seas, which cover 70 percent of the earth's surface. It is the developed countries mainly that have the technology to use these seas and their pelagic floors efficiently for shipping, for fishing (often to excess with the extinction of useful species), for the production of offshore oil, for the harvesting of minerals, such as manganese nodules containing copper and lead as well as manganese.

Each one of these items could be developed at length to illumine and illustrate the need for a greater measure of real interdependence among the inhabitants of a shrinking planet

with growing needs. Absent such considerations in any present workable form—even though discussions are finally in
progress on all of these subjects—I do not find it surprising
that many thoughtful earth dwellers are losing heart, that we
are witnessing a whole spate of pessimistic and doomsday
predictions. Yet, I am not a prophet of gloom and doom.
Neither am I a Micawber who believes that somehow everything will get better and turn out all right. It will get better, I
believe, but only if we can change profoundly, only if interdependence passes from an idea to a fruitful and operative
reality in the political, economic, and social life of the whole
planet.

We in the West have created, in short order as history runs,
a world of incredible global discontinuities and injustices. For
example, one could always sense racial prejudices, but today
billions of people are automatically and uncontrollably suffering geographic prejudice. If a child is born in the north, he or
she faces an ever-lengthening life characterized by increasing
health, education, economic and social well-being. If born in
most of the southern parts of our globe, he or she will face a
short life, illness, illiteracy, hunger, abominable housing,
hopelessness. We in the northern part of this globe worry
about overproducing Ph.D.'s; many children in the Southern
Hemisphere never enter a school. We speak of heart and
kidney transplants; they never see a doctor from birth to
death. Half the children already born in the poorest countries
will die before the age of five. We are often overfed and
overweight; they are undernourished from birth, often suffering brain damage therefrom. We speak often of second
homes; they live in cardboard or mud and wattle huts. We
travel anywhere on earth, now supersonically, in hours; they
are trapped for a miserable lifetime in urban or rural slums.
We spend more annually on foolish armaments, devilishly
devised to destroy life, than they have annually available to
maintain life.

And yet, we all are fellow travelers aboard a common
spacecraft, ever more intimately interdependent. The decision of an Arab sheik, a Japanese industrialist, an American
governmental bureaucrat leaves them without irrigation

water and fertilizer and, consequently, without food. A decision between the great powers to end the Cold War removes the one foolish reason that motivated a substantial part of the aid they received—so aid starts diminishing drastically just when the need is greatest.

Even so, if I had to characterize my own position, it would be one of Christian and cautious optimism. Theologically, I have good reasons for Christian optimism. It is my reading of the unwillingness of the affluent and powerful of this world to change, to begin to think interdependently, that makes me cautious. It is my hope that if we develop a new world view, really understand our current situation on this troubled planet, we will begin to create a better world as the new millennium approaches.

I would hope that we might indeed create new, interdependent, worldwide socioeconomic relations, and new political ones, too. Rather than simply looking at the difficulties and limitations of our capacities for response, I would prefer to look at the new opportunities and creative responses that interdependence would suggest. Human ingenuity in the face of crisis has been one of mankind's greatest glories.

Sometimes a picture is worth a million words. Take our view of the earth from the moon, which reduces the size of our spacecraft. Instead of 4 billion people, difficult to imagine, think of a crew of five persons, each representing a segment of humanity. The person representing us and our world, mostly Judeo-Christian, white, Western, affluent, has the use of 80 percent of the available life resources and amenities aboard our spacecraft. The other four crew members must share the 20 percent that is left. The situation, though inequitous and unjust, is still deteriorating. Our crewman is increasing his share to 90 percent at the moment, leaving 2½ percent for each of the other crew members.

Now I ask you—given the fundamental interdependence of a spacecraft's crew—can you imagine much lasting peace or order or good life aboard this spacecraft? The other crew members are not just uneasy and frustrated, they are outraged, as well as hungry and hopeless, since our person also seems to have the only lethal weapon aboard. If our person, we ourselves, does not begin to perceive the utter injustice of the situation, and begin to organize the use of these finite resources in a more just fashion, he will ultimately, inevitably, be overwhelmed by some manner of violence. It is no chance affair that one of the most troubled nations of all has recently developed an atomic bomb.

My thesis is that we have every theological, philosophical, and humane imperative to change, to respond, and we can find creative ways of doing so. And we must, if we wish peace, as well as survival. At this juncture, I believe I should advance some concrete proposals so that you do not think me a utopian dreamer or impractical theologian.

For interdependence to become a central concern in the Western world, somehow it must be related to the key theological and philosophical principles that characterize our culture today.

1. *Theologically*, we might begin by answering the question of Cain in the book of Genesis: "Am I my brother's keeper?" I hope we answer yes, especially since our Lord gave us a most specific mandate: "Whatsoever you do for these, my least brethren, you do for *me*." No discontinuity here and no question who are our least brethren in today's world. The choices are simple and stark: greed or altruism, hatred or love, growing discontinuities or new development, in short, war or peace.

Beyond these specific imperatives, it seems to me that the movement to ecumenism in our times, new understanding between and among Christians of various Christian churches first, and then a broader religious understanding between Christians and non-Christians, is a most important underpinning for unity among the great majority of earth dwellers who believe in God—first the sons of Abraham: Muslims, Jews, and Christians; and then the other great religions of the world: Hindus, Confucianists, Buddhists, Shintoists, animists, and others. Nothing cements world dwellers together so much as belief in a supreme being who has established a moral order binding on all of us who believe in him, whatever we call him. The disregard of that moral order today is at the root of our problems.

2. *Philosophically*, the unity of mankind is best manifested in our times by a new commitment to human dignity and human rights, to be observed always and everywhere. The United Nations Universal Declaration of Human Rights, spelled out twenty-five years ago under the leadership of Eleanor Roosevelt and Réné Cassin, was indeed a high mark of declaration that in our day must be ever more matched by reality—even though all will admit we are yet far from the mark. Interdependence will be meaningless until we show in practice that justice to men and women and children everywhere is our goal, and injustice anywhere by anyone will meet with condemnation by the human community. We are far from achieving this goal, but at least I take it that we have agreed on the road map.

3. *The material realities* of food, housing, and health are important because they provide the indispensable material context within which human dignity may be a reality and not a travesty. As one who has worked for more than a decade with the Rockefeller Foundation on the Green Revolution, I can assure you that the world can feed itself if it really decides to do so. Population growth will have to level off because the net addition of 70 million people a year puts an intolerable burden on possible and probable agricultural productivity advances. Actually, every developed country controls its population, so that development and population strategies must go hand-in-hand. But this can be done if mankind determines to do it. It is much less difficult than putting a man on the moon, and we have done that.

4. *Teaching technologies.* There are more illiterates today than twenty years ago. But during these years, we have developed technologies that now make it possible to teach everyone in the world—using the best of teachers and the latest teaching techniques. This involves synchronous satellites, miniaturized data banks, computers, television, miniaturized atomic energy, xerography, various other techniques. But all are at hand. We have only to use them to create a university of the world. I use university here in its broadest sense: comprising access to the vast storehouse of human knowledge, science, and art through literacy and, in

addition, access to all those practical arts and sciences and technologies that are indispensable to mankind's total human and personal development. I believe we are suffering worldwide urbanization today, with all its dire human miseries, because the rural areas are so isolated and deathly dull. A university of the world through worldwide free television could change this, just as your university without walls has enriched the lives and the possibilities of so many of your people.

5. *The political organization* of the world would seem nonsensical to anyone visiting us from outer space. As Lord Franks said many years ago, our present problem is not East and West, but North and South. I would suggest a triregional global North-South configuration for future development. The three North-South regions would be the Orient; Europe, including Russia and its satellites, the Middle East and Africa; and, thirdly, the Western Hemisphere. The northern components of these regions, in my projection, would be interested in developing the resources south of them—the developed teamed up with the underdeveloped, the strong strengthening the weak with an infusion of capital and technology, with the multinational corporations perhaps being most helpful in the process.

6. *The multinational corporation.* Multinational corporations, even though viewed quite negatively and with great suspicion by many developing nations today, are engines for world development. In fact, multinationals, or transnationals as they are sometimes called, are an impressive interdependent reality in today's world, although some think that they highlight dependency verging on exploitation and political interference at times. Of the 100 largest economic entities in the world, 58 are sovereign nations and 42 are multinational corporations. General Motors is larger than Switzerland, Pakistan, or South Africa. The combined sales of the multinationals top $400 billion, more than 10 percent of the global gross national product and still growing. While most of the multinationals' investment is in industrial countries, a growing amount is in developing nations. For example, of the United States multinationals' cumulative direct overseas investment

of $94 billion, $17 billion was invested in Latin America.

One should admit that the experience of multinationals in developing countries has been mixed, both positive and negative, depending on the company and the country. It is quite possible now to devise a tentative set of conditions that would clearly make the multinational corporation an engine of development, an agent of social justice in an interdependent world even greater than country-to-country relationships, since the multinational has greater freedom of action and greater mobility, sometimes even greater vision.

First, the multinational has capital and technological expertise that the developing country desperately needs and could pay for out of new profits.

Second, the multinational can pick the best developing country for a given product and assure good markets for its delivery and sale.

Third, the multinational could assure at least 51 percent ownership of the local enterprise in the developing country. This is also the best insurance against nationalization and expropriation.

Fourth, the multinational could develop a new, developing-country technology that is labor intensive rather than capital intensive, and could train nationals for every level of work and management.

Lastly, multinationals could also consider regional development and work for agricultural, as well as industrial, progress.

If these five conditions were observed, both the multinational and the host developing country would prosper together.

To return now to my triregional perspective, I would not see this as impeding normal East-West trade relationships, but at least each region would deal with the other totally and from a position of strength. In the political order, certainly this triregional arrangement would be better than the present foolish situation in the United Nations, with almost 150 nations, ranging in size from China to Gambia, each having an equal vote. Each of the three regions would come together economically more easily than politically, but eventually a triregional political alignment, however loose, would be more rational, especially in liberating for regional and world development the enormous financial and technological resources now wasted on foolish armaments.

The greatest enemy to all of these proposals is nationalism, a kind of historical insanity that deeply afflicts us all. Rather than fight nationalism lodged so deeply in our bones, I would prefer to bypass it. What I am suggesting is that each human being be given the option of dual citizenship. All are, in fact, citizens of the country in which they were born. Why not give everyone the additional option, in this largely interdependent world, of opting for dual citizenship—world citizenship, in addition to national citizenship?

Everyone opting for world citizenship would have to produce some evidence of his dedication to world justice and peace, some perception of the interdependence of all mankind on spaceship earth today. I think all of us will be surprised to see how many of the younger generation will opt for dual citizenship and work for global justice. This expectation, I trust not vain, is one of my main reasons for personal hope today and for world peace tomorrow.